D0948611

Penguin Special

**Because They're Black**

Derek Humphry was born in Somerset, England,
in 1930. He began in journalism at fifteen as a
messenger in the London office of the *Yorkshire
Post*, then became a junior reporter on the *Bristol
Evening World*. He completed his training with the
*Manchester Evening News* and spent six years with
the *Daily Mail*. He edited a local weekly newspaper
for three years and left to join the *Sunday Times*,
for which he specializes in reporting on race
relations and civil rights matters, and investigating
rackets.

Gus John was born in Grenada, West Indies, in
1945. He studied philosophy and theology in
Trinidad from 1962 to 1964. He then came to
England and continued to study theology at
Blackfriars, Oxford, where he did sociology and
social anthropology as subsidiary subjects. After
Oxford he went to London in 1968, where he
worked as an unattached youth worker in
Paddington and Notting Hill. In 1969 he took the
Diploma in Youth Work at the National College
for the Training of Youth Leaders, Leicester.
He is now engaged in an action research group
project with the Youth Development Trust,
Manchester.

Gus John and
Derek Humphry

# Because
# They're
# Black

 Penguin Books

DA 125
.A1 J57

Penguin Books Ltd, Harmondsworth,
Middlesex, England
Penguin Books Inc., 7110 Ambassador Road,
Baltimore, Maryland 21207, U.S.A.
Penguin Books Australia Ltd, Ringwood,
Victoria, Australia

First published 1971
Copyright © Gus John, Derek Humphry, 1971

Made and printed in Great Britain by
C. Nicholls & Company Ltd
Set in Monotype Times

This book is sold subject to the condition that
it shall not, by way of trade or otherwise, be lent,
re-sold, hired out, or otherwise circulated without
the publisher's prior consent in any form of
binding or cover other than that in which it is
published and without a similar condition
including this condition being imposed on the
subsequent purchaser

INDIANA
PURDUE
LIBRARY
JAN    1972

WITHDRAWN

FORT WAYNE

# Contents

FEB 8 1972

# Acknowledgement

The authors are indebted to the *Sunday Times* and the Runnymede Trust, for permission to use material gathered on their behalf for part of this book. Both wish to acknowledge their gratitude to Mr Harold Evans, editor of the *Sunday Times*, and Mr Dipak Nandy, Director of Runnymede, for their personal support and advice.

# 1. How it looks from inside

*Gus John writes:* I was a secret observer on the people of my race during the winter of 1969–70. It was not a role I relished but it was necessary, if someone was to look deeply and objectively into the sudden decline in racial harmony in Handsworth, Birmingham, to operate incognito. The Runnymede Trust, an independent foundation which provides information and promotes public education on race relations, picked me, a stranger to the area, to provide a rapid if limited guide to the situation of a multi-racial inner-city area.

In the summer of 1969 a West Indian youth was stabbed in Handsworth Park. That incident brought to a head a growing concern about violence, crime and the breakdown of law and order which had been building up for some years. At the same time complaints from West Indians of a marked deterioration in the treatment they received from the police also grew in volume. Clearly, if it was important to try to discover who was right, it was even more important to uncover the basic problems of the area.

But there was another reason for choosing Handsworth. It is in many ways a typical inner-city suburb, once prosperous, now on the decline, and multi-racial. In the eyes of many of its older residents that decline is associated with the arrival of black immigrants, although the facts do not support that view. To the blacks, on the other hand, Handsworth is a kind of second-class area to which 'the second slaves' (as one West Indian resident put it) are relegated. Handsworth is not unique or peculiarly nasty but it is in so many ways typical of the inner areas of our major cities – areas suffering neglect and decay. Sometimes these areas are all-white, sometimes they are multi-racial. In the latter case, the problems frequently manifest themselves in terms of racial tension and sometimes in increased tension between the police and groups within the community. There is, moreover, some reason to believe that the problems of such areas are significantly different from the problems of traditional working-class slum neighbourhoods. Handsworth, and areas like it, are not the Gorbals or the East End before the war. If this view were correct, there would be a considerable difference in the approach of the police, of social workers, of planners, to areas like Handsworth.

I was three months 'under cover' in Handsworth, moving among blacks of all classes and ages, living with them, drinking with them, and after the *Sunday Times* published a summary of my findings I was out in the open and spent another six months in Handsworth trying to help those who were struggling. I managed to assist a few, disappointed many others, and wrote a report on Handsworth which was sent to the Home Office. I tried to influence it so that it would allocate more money to Handsworth and look more positively at its commitment to similar areas.

My work wasn't a copper-bottomed, methodologically impeccable study of the total situation. In it I tried to give the black people a chance to voice *their* view of *their* situation. We seem to be overwhelmed with academic social science on race relations, using the market research approach and doing little more than quantify the obvious. While I am among the first to recognize the limitations of an impressionistic study, I also feel it necessary to emphasize that what people think in a situation such as that in Handsworth is of utmost importance. It both determines their stance to society and motivates their actions. Dare we dismiss lightly their interpretation of the situation?

At 6.30 every week-day morning a stream of women pass along Grove Lane and Rookery Lane, Handsworth, clutching the hands of sleepy-eyed kids. They vanish into various houses, emerge childless, smooth their coats from the rumpling of the farewell hug, pat their hair, and hurry off in the direction of the factories, office blocks and restaurants. To see this simple operation of transfer of human beings is to witness the ghetto syndrome at its birth. These are men and women who have come from

Britain's old colonies to try to make a better living for themselves – the new British working class.

Syndrome was once an exclusively medical term meaning 'a combination of various symptoms of a disease'. Now it is used in everyday language, yet its original medical definition has a disturbing meaning when the term 'ghetto syndrome' is used. From the dismal days as a toddler in a child-minder's house up to working life the black person must struggle. Some have the ability to stand, suffer and survive; some crack up; the lucky few who escape will be marked for life.

The typical black child lives with his parents in one or two rooms, usually high up or low down, in a house containing many families, and has little room to play. Because his mother must join the father in earning enough to live the child has to be looked after during the day. He is herded with six to twelve others in a paraffin-heated room and from Monday to Friday knows no mother love, enjoys no personal attention, never learns from communication and play. At night his mother collects him and puts him to bed early so that she may relax. Her week-ends are spent shopping, cleaning, relaxing. When the ghetto child starts school at five he often seems duller than others: shy, introverted, with a poor vocabulary blurred by dialect and his behavioural pattern confused by the strange life he has led in two homes. He has known two disciplinary codes, and now must adjust to a third at school – that of the white race and middle class. He is prone to be labelled 'problem child', especially by reception teachers unaware of the situations from which children come to them.

Education is one of the fields in which the problems of a poor area (the stresses on an immigrant community, the increased sharpness with which the normal inter-generational conflicts are felt in such a community, and the problems of colour) focus themselves most clearly. There are still many parents who believe that education only starts when the child enters school, but a key factor is adequate preparation for school, and with its over-crowding, lack of play-space, high percentage of working mothers, Handsworth has a lot of deprived kids in this respect.

If the toddlers fresh out of the child-minders' clutches have problems, they are no bigger than those of the kids who have come to England when they are between ten and fourteen. Eighty such children I talked to were worried about the fact that their achievements were not very great by English standards. They were all apprehensive about the prospect of finding jobs, and were prepared to postpone the evil day as long as possible. Most anticipated a battle with employers and with the Youth Employment Service if they were to get decent jobs. Some saw their future as a process of being ground down and were unwilling to accept it with resignation.

I talked to about 200 kids and about two-thirds felt they were being taught a great deal about Britain and British standards and values and not enough about other cultures. Most felt that opportunities were being missed in subjects like history, geography, literature and religious instruction or discussing other cultures. The educational scene in Handsworth is depressing, as you can see from some of the things the kids told me which appear later in the book. Only a detailed study could show just how bad things are. Do we have the courage to look?

Out of school hours the youngsters have almost nowhere to go. They feel hemmed in. A lot of youngsters ridiculed the idea of youth clubs. There aren't enough of them anyway, the kids don't consider those that exist to be the right type offering what they (and not the management committees) see as relevant recreational facilities. To many whom I found in youth clubs it was either the only place they could go, or the only place their parents would let them go. Past and present members complained of authoritarian and paternalistic youth leaders and club structures. They wanted a more unstructured setting within which they could promote more spontaneous activity. But one youth leader told me he had tried the free-for-all approach, only to produce complaints that the club was boring and not enough was happening. It came to a state where members said they came to the club because they would rather be there than at home, not because they liked the club. The only real club in the area – at least in summer – is Handsworth Park. Hundreds of youngsters use the park in fine weather, especially when the schools and clubs are closed.

The beginnings of the path to crime are almost always to be found in a broken home. A product of the old colonial slave society is that many West Indians contract several unions in their early adult life and the children of these liaisons face harrowing family problems due to economic pressures in the Caribbean. Often they join their parents in Britain after a long separation; perhaps it is only one parent – they may not get on well with the other one. As they grow up they fail to harmonize at home and soon leave. The generation gap often grows into an unbreachable abyss due to widely differing values and expectations. So many older blacks are content to live a plain, subdued life which is quite unacceptable to the teenagers. The number of young men and women leaving home before they can stand on their own feet financially is increasing, and hostels, at least as a stop-gap measure, are desperately needed to catch them on the rebound before they are swallowed up by the ghetto's criminal traps, or fall into prostitution.

Jobs are the biggest source of discontent and bitterness, although statistically the situation does not appear bad at all. I interviewed thirty-five youngsters under twenty who had been unemployed for over three months, and another seventy who had been helped to find jobs by the Youth Employment Bureau. The successful boys were grateful to the service for its efforts but from them, as from the thirty-five unemployed, the major criticism was not so much that they could not find jobs as that the jobs did not conform either to their abilities or to what they particularly wanted to do. While the overall statistics show a relatively low unemployment rate amongst black youngsters, these statistics mask the severe degree of job-dissatisfaction. No one should make judgements about youngsters who kick over the traces and get into trouble with the authorities, until they have considered what the world looks like to today's youngster who has nothing in front of him except the prospect of forty or fifty years as an unskilled labourer.

The stress and conflict within the community leads to wild talk about 'violent black men' and 'delinquent immigrants' by the whites. To hear the talk one would think most blacks were crooks. One police official put the number of criminal types and delinquents – he called them 'the hard core' – at between forty and fifty. There are about 10,000 blacks in Handsworth. A number of other youths get taken to court, fined, put on probation or given other punishments and the police pay particular attention to these if their offences are in any way connected with individuals who belong to 'the hard core'. Handsworth is a short bus ride from the city centre. Black and white tearaways from all over Birmingham pay the area regular visits for kicks and swell the number of troublemakers. Young lads doing a boring job for small pay are easy prey for the older man, who points out to him that his grandparents were slaves under British rule, and his parents are barely eking out an existence here. The black man is only wanted for cheap labour by white society, he says (and is he far wrong?), and soon the youngster gives up trying. One more for the hustlers.

Disillusionment, discontent, embitterment are pretty rampant among the young people for most of the foregoing reasons. Many of them are showing anger and militancy. Very few are resigned to their situation. Existing as they do against a mountain of odds, it is astonishing that relatively few resort to violence or crime. And herein lies another trap. The Establishment are quick to point out that it is only a few blacks who are violent or crooks, and maintains that the rest of them are perfectly content with their life, enjoying the benefits of Britain's sophisticated society, high standard of living and the welfare state. They see the problem of social discontent merely as one of law and order. But huge numbers of law-abiding blacks say things can't go on as they are much longer. They worry about the kids and their futures; they worry about Powellism and the spectre of repatriation.

The police station in Thornhill Road is the building most dreaded and hated by black Handsworth. It is the symbol of white oppression. They talk of 'the pigs at Thornhill Road' or 'Babylon House' or 'the place where thugs hang out'. A frightening state of conflict. Mutual confidence between the blacks and the police appears to have broken down in two stages. The first phase, starting in the early 1960s, saw the police trying to stamp out petty pilfering, car-breaking, shoplifting and similar offences on the one hand, and the so-called 'big jobs' on the other. The police believed then, as they do now, that gangs of black men engaged in organized crimes in Handsworth and made this their only mode of subsistence. They were very vigilant and scrutinized the activities of every black man whom they knew to be out of work, or whom they saw hanging around clubs, coffee bars, betting offices. This meant that they often quizzed people who had no part in crime, had never been involved with the police, and who prided themselves as ordinary, good-living citizens. In their zeal the police antagonized many people and left the impression that they regarded black men and youths in Handsworth generally as natural or potential criminals. This engendered a tremendous amount of resentment which manifested itself the moment the police approached a black man, no matter how legitimate the approach.

The second phase began with events subsequent to the incident in Handsworth Park in 1969 when a West Indian youth was accidentally stabbed and died as a result. Since it happened while a group of youngsters were playing with knives, the police and the public were concerned about the number of black youngsters who went around carrying knives or other offensive weapons. After the death of that lad there were many comments in the local newspapers by black community leaders, by police representatives and by journalists on black youths in Handsworth. One article which had probably most impact, by Brian Priestley, assistant editor of the *Birmingham Evening Mail*, was pointedly headlined *The bitter young men of Handsworth*. A West Indian youth worker, with responsibility for detached work, who is often spoken of as one of the most dependable members of the black community, made it his business to comment in the press and to call a meeting of youth and community leaders to discuss the situation after the stabbing. He recommended to the youth leaders that they pronounce an amnesty in their clubs and give the youngsters a certain number of days in which to hand in their knives or weapons. Moreover, he went around Handsworth with policemen of varied ranks in uniform and in plain clothes telling the youngsters in the park, on street corners and in cafés of the dangers of carrying knives and coaxing them into handing their weapons over to the police. On the face of it this seemed a laudable idea but it met with little or no success and resulted in his being one of the most resented men in Handsworth. At a later consultation with the police he recommended that each youngster be disarmed of his weapons, even if it meant searching everyone and prosecuting those found with knives for carrying offensive weapons. The police welcomed this plan and proceeded to execute it. They therefore, in their own words, 'put the pressure on' for a few weeks and few youths or men escaped being stopped and searched, especially late at night. Once again the majority were being harassed because of the sins of the few. Would such blanket checking be done among a white population in a similar situation? I doubt it. Many observers of the criminal scene whom I have asked also doubt it.

Young people told me that they felt the police went much too far in their pressure. They saw it as racial harassment. The boys allege that in some cases black men were planted with drugs, knives and screwdrivers. Around this time the Recorder at the City's Quarter Sessions court remarked that he was getting very concerned about the number of black men from Handsworth appearing before the courts. Yet it is very significant that even at that peak period, police statistics show that the number of offences committed by black men in Handsworth – or perhaps more accurately the number of black men prosecuted – was proportionately much lower than that of the rest of the community generally. But black men in Handsworth continued to be the major cause for concern, and police pressure escalated. To this day resentment of police by blacks and resentment of blacks by police continues to grow. When one talks to police superintendents, inspectors and sergeants they generally deny any allegation of police maltreatment, but recently at least two superintendents have been admitting to me, however inadvertently, that the man on the beat is guided not only by the rulebook but also by his attitudes.

Not a week went by during my nine months in Handsworth without my hearing of at least one instance of someone being taken, or having to go, to hospital for treatment as a result of injuries sustained at the hands of the police. Youths and their parents complain about the police's indiscriminate use of handcuffs, of police insults to black women who they regard as 'only black and therefore not to be respected as women', of men being put against the walls of the police station and searched, at the same time being asked 'Where are the drugs, you dirty black bastard?', 'You don't work, you scum', 'You live off our women', 'I am going to make damn sure you will get put inside for good.' Many blacks complain of police fabricating charges and 'piling them on', by which they mean an offence which could be a minor charge justifying a fine being developed into a major charge carrying a prison sentence.

The relationship between the police and black men in Handsworth is one of war, and not a cold war. Certain police officials are extremely concerned about this clash and are thinking of positive measures to end it. But they always hasten to emphasize that the police are sticking their necks out, since it is not their business to be concerned with social problems. They respond to community needs, they say, and it is their duty to preserve law and order, regardless of symptoms and causes. They argue that people should be able to walk the streets of Handsworth day and night without fear of having their handbags taken, of being coshed and robbed, of being raped and molested. And if it is brought to their attention that this is not the case, then it is the duty of the police to intervene and make sure that it is possible. The police want to see more school premises made available for youth clubs and a beginning to youth clubs run by the police. I doubt whether either would work. Youngsters are loath to 'go back to school' for their evening's entertainment and, given the existing police image, a centre staffed by policemen would only be ridiculed. Many points of view on this come later in the book.

In 1967 and 1968 America was wracked by racial riots in which people died, many were terribly injured, and a great deal of property was damaged. President Johnson set up a special commission to investigate the causes. The findings of the US Riot Commission report, which was probably the most far-reaching, intensive and outspoken social document of our times (it also became a best-selling book), include many points relevant to my study. The report said:

The abrasive relationship between the police and the minority communities has been a major – and explosive – source of grievance, tension and disorder. *The blame must be shared by the total society* [my italics]. The police are faced with demands for increased protection and service in the ghetto. Yet the aggressive patrol practices, though necessary to meet these demands, themselves create tension and hostility. . . . The police are not merely the 'spark' factor. To some Negroes police have come to symbolize white power, white racism and white repression. And the fact is that many police do reflect and express these white attitudes. The atmosphere of hostility and cynicism is reinforced by a widespread belief among Negroes of the existence of police brutality and in a 'double standard' of justice and protection – one for Negroes and one for whites. . . . The typical rioter was a teen-ager or young adult, a lifelong resident of the city in which he rioted, a high school dropout; he was nevertheless somewhat better educated than his non-rioting Negro neighbour and was usually under-employed or employed in a menial job. He was proud of his race, extremely hostile to whites and middle-class Negroes, and, although informed about politics, highly distrustful of the political system.

After the Ulster riots between Roman Catholics and Protestants, our own student troubles, and the few racial incidents we have so far had in this country, can any sincere person doubt that the American findings have a lesson for us? My co-author and I do not join with Enoch Powell in predicting 'a nation busily engaged in heaping up its own funeral pyre' but we do say that trouble is coming in the 1970s unless we act fast to improve the social conditions. The poor quality of local government and the preponderance of white racism make rapid action almost impossible in the USA. In Britain we have perhaps the world's most highly developed governmental system with wealth to support it; all that is needed is the will to spend the money and make the effort. To that end we have written this book.

## 2. Tell it like it is

'He passed an aptitude test for a Royal Navy commission but was told that a coloured officer would be bad for discipline. So he got the message that his colour was going to be a handicap, and after going to live with a Stepney girl because he was lonely he met East End thieves and turned into a criminal.' – *Mr Roger Frisby* QC, *defending ex-fairground boxer Mark Owens, 35, who received 18 months' jail for his part in the Parkhurst prison riot in October 1969.* 'I accept that you have been bruised by your unhappy experience of colour prejudice,' *the judge told him.*

*

'An officer of the department was investigating a complaint that two Anglo-Pakistani boys were not receiving adequate food. The complaint upon investigation proved unjustified but the child care officer found himself confronted with the problem of three Pakistanis – two men and one woman – slowly starving to death. The two men had lost their jobs several months previously, had been unable to obtain others and were too proud to obtain help either through the employment exchange or the social security services. All they lived on was some meal they purchased with the one child's family allowance. After this was finished they had no food for the rest of the week.' – *From a child welfare department confidential report on immigrants: to Birmingham city council, February 1970.*

*

*Mr Sindh Kartar, grandfather of a two-month old Birmingham girl who died from pneumonia and toxo-plasmosis, caused by rat bites:* 'When are they going to rehouse us? They have knocked down all the houses which the Europeans used to live in but they have done nothing about the old houses occupied by the Indians and Pakistanis.' *The deputy Medical Officer of Health said:* 'We are not always successful in getting through to the immigrants. We do all we can to encourage them to report the presence of rats but in this case we definitely had no notification that there were rats in the house.'

*

*Anthea Disney, a girl reporter who turned her skin black with drugs to find out how coloured people live in Handsworth, Birmingham:* 'Why then do people turn to look at me in this city where the coloured faces of Indians, Pakistanis and West Indians are hardly rare? At first I think, uncomfortably, that it is because they see me as an imposter, as a white girl in fancy dress and a sun tan. Then I realize they stare blatantly at several coloured people. It seems that, because I am coloured, I am expected not to see – or not to mind – their blank-faced curiosity. At moments I feel like shouting: For God's sake, I'm British and as white as you are. How dare you look at me like that. As though I have no feelings. As though I am a creature apart. My husband, who came to visit me in Birmingham, took me to a dinner-dance at the Albany, the smartest hotel in the area. I wore a sari and although no one snubbed me and despite his reassuring presence, half-way through the meal he said to me: "You're behaving differently. You've changed. You are acting like an under-privileged person and looking hunted." I suddenly realized he was right. My confidence was gone. It has been sapped by several weeks of cool white resentment.' *From her story in the* Daily Sketch.

*

*George Tonkin, a Welshman whose skin turned brown through a kidney disease:* 'Suddenly Britain and even my home town had become places where if I walked on the streets I faced insults. Where if I went into a pub, I risked being snubbed. Where if I went for a job there were automatically no vacancies. I became one of those men who some people love to hate. I had become a coloured man. Since the change of colour I can feel a change in my personality. I have become more wary and withdrawn. I have to be on my guard all the time. Because of my colour I go as little as possible to London. If I do I go by car. I've read about this Paki-bashing. I hate going on tubes and buses just in case there's a skinhead ready to put the boot in. I know my fears are probably not justified. But I now realize that these are the same fears thousands of coloured people living in Britain have every day.' *From Mr Tonkin's own story in the* News of the World.

Tonkin died in December 1970 following a kidney-transplant operation which he hoped would turn him white again. He was thirty-one.

*

*Two Jamaicans at a party:* 'My engagement party was given by my fiancée's mother at her home in W9. Fifteen minutes after midnight I saw about six or eight policemen in the hallway. One walked up the stairs and opened my jacket and searched me and said "You're not the one we are looking for." My future mother-in-law and my fiancée who were with me and I went downstairs and I saw about six of them beating up Charlie. I saw a policeman breaking up the coffee table on the landing. I told him that he should not do that and he turned around and hit me with his truncheon over my head and then took me to the van. Before I left the house I saw the policeman throw the dressing table over in the children's bedroom. While I was in the van I saw them bring out Septimus and they were beating him while they were bringing him out with their truncheons and threw him in the van. While I was in the van I heard a policeman say "Why don't you go back to your country, you black bastard." When we reached the station the policemen were roughing us up and pushing us around. I was charged and put in a cell and a doctor came in and cleaned up my head. I was released and went to hospital where I was X-rayed and received about four stitches in my head. I have never been in trouble with the police before.' *Signed statement.*

'I and my wife were invited to my aunt's engagement party. There were many guests and we played records, danced and had food and drink. At about 12.15 a.m. I was just coming down the stairs and I saw the front door open and three policemen came in. I asked them what they wanted and one of them said: "It's always the black bastards who cause the trouble." I told them that they had no right entering the premises without a warrant and one of them said "Shut your fucking cakehole." Then I called him "Bighead". When I called him that he was about to go through the front door; he turned and came back toward me and I ran through to the kitchen and he chased me. I opened the kitchen window and climbed out and entered another door that led upstairs. He caught me in an upstairs room – two of them grabbed hold of me, and I went with them down the stairs and entered the police van. When we reached the police station they dragged my brother out of the van and I followed him in. My brother was already in the room and I could see the policemen beating him. Then I went to my brother and tried to help him because I had seen a policeman hit him in the cut with a truncheon and on his head. He was kicked and punched. When I got near my brother I was hit over the head and another two kicked my knees. I was on the floor by this time and another one kicked me on my neck. I remembered no more. I think I must have been knocked out. When I came to, two policemen helped me to stand up. I was then charged, put in a cell, and asked if I wanted to see the doctor. The doctor examined me and put some lotion on the back of my ear. I was later released. I have a small cut inside my left cheek, two scratches on my left outside wrist, one cut on my right knee, a large scratch and bruises on my left shin. My left cheek bone is very swollen. I have never been in trouble with the police before.' *Signed statement.*

\*

*Police Superintendent Kenneth Johnson with responsibility to promote police/blacks liaison in Birmingham:* 'If only people would realize that policemen are human beings behind this uniform, and that the policeman's lot is really a wretched one. When the man on the beat sees his colleague coming back to the station with a nose broken, his face bashed in, looking a real sorry mess, do you think he could go out there and as soon as he goes up to a black man receives nothing but insults and total lack of cooperation, and yet not be firm?'

\*

*Under the heading* God is not a landlord, *the* Guardian *published this letter on 26 March 1970:* 'I am a young American journalist residing in London. Recently I took a flat in a large, centrally-located building. I told the caretaker I had a respectable, well-educated friend coming from the US to share the flat. I didn't think it necessary (in Britain) to mention that he is a Negro. Everything was set. When he arrived I took him to meet the caretaker. After a momentary loss of composure the usually smiling Irish woman took me aside. She said: "You didn't tell me the boy was coloured. I'm not prejudiced, but the landlord doesn't want any coloured people here. I believe that we are *all* God's children." After much persuasion we have been allowed "a few weeks" to find another place. When I told my friend he showed little reaction but went out "for a walk".

There is an article (*Nixon's appalling race record*) in a recent issue of the *New Statesman*. It begins: *Integration of black and white – once America's proudest goal – is being methodically smashed*. Another magazine has on its cover in bold type: *America: A dream gone sour*. Recent experience reinforces my belief that ethics, justice and equality belong to individuals, not to countries.' *J. M. Freels*.

\*

*Mrs X, an Englishwoman standing at a bus-stop:* 'I have lived in Handsworth for fifty years. I was born here. I inherited my father's property. Handsworth is no longer a place to be proud of. This used to be one of the nicest areas in Birmingham. We have this lovely park there and I am afraid to go and sit in it. I used to spend many hours in the park but now with all these darkies running around there you never know what they would do to you, do you? The first lot of your people who came were quite all right really, but now there seem to be so many young men about day and night with nothing to do. They make Handsworth what it is now. And of course there's all this talk about crime. I am afraid to walk the streets. I think it is terrible, and the police are not doing enough about it.'

\*

*Mr Jones, a white man in a Handsworth pub:* 'No, I wasn't born here but I have lived here twenty-three years. It's changed a lot you know. Of course I saw lots of white people move out. Most of my friends think I am barmy for staying. But I don't mind black people. I know a few of them where I work and some round where I live. I have never felt I wanted to move out. Your people take accommodation where they can get it, and if white people move out then it's obvious they're going to buy those houses and the schools will have lots of black children. Of course there's very little in the area for the young ones. A lot of them get into trouble.'

\*

*Marcus, a nineteen-year-old Jamaican:* 'This place is a dump. There is nothing for a young fellow like me to do. I never go near youth clubs – they're just not my scene. Some of the leaders are twits. You're in school and you get treated like kids. You're at home and you get treated like kids. You go to the youth club and you get treated like kids. I'm sure some lads go there for want of something better to do. Still, some of them run the oc-casional groovy disco. It's hell to be young in Handsworth. No matter how good you try to be people still think you're bad. You can't walk the streets in peace without some bloody cop trying to pry and search you, or some white guys trying to do you, especially at night when you're alone. Man, you just got to know how to defend yourself. Because some black guys get into trouble the cops and everyone else seem to think that all young blacks are criminals. That really niggles me.'

\*

*A West Indian father of four, who works for British Rail:* 'Hands-worth is a difficult place to live in. At least my friends keep me going. Man, all you seem to do in this place is work, work, and no matter how hard you work you never seem to have anything to show for it. It's hell to bring up children in Handsworth. As things are today you have to keep your eyes open all the time to make sure they don't get into trouble. They don't like me keeping them in but it is the only way. There are some white boys living near us. I know they don't like my big boy and I don't want them ganging up on him. No doubt when you have been here longer you will see how vile this place is.'

\*

*A black mother, domestic staff member at a hospital:* 'My mind is more at rest when I know that my child is being cared for by Mrs X, whom I know and who has kept two other children for me, than by the people at the day nursery.'

\*

*Black boys and girls at secondary modern schools:*
'If you don't push yourself and try to be one-up on everybody else, you haven't got a hope in hell.'

'Man, those teachers just don't care. School is a bind. Teachers not only think you're stupid but the sort of things they teach you make you yourself believe that you're stupid. I think some of them are just born racialist.'

'The teachers in my school need to be sitting in with the class and being taught. We seem to be landed with a load of teachers who have just got through their teacher training. Sometimes I wonder how some of them did it. You talk to some of my mates over there. I am sure they would tell you the same thing. I think they deliberately send second-rate teachers into Handsworth; and then they turn round and say because there are so many black kids in the school the standard of education is being lowered.'

'Brother, don't let anyone fool you. All these teachers are trying to do is to keep you down. When the time comes for us to think of choosing jobs they always say we aim too high. They know they deliberately didn't teach us a damn thing and they even tell some of us we're going to end up on the factory floor or on the buses. They got a hope!'

\*

*Fifteen-year-old Jamaican girl sharing flat with nineteen-year-old brother:* 'I took my eleven-plus three months after I came to this country from Jamaica. I did well in everything else except history and so I failed. I tried learning up everything in history as quickly as I could before the exam, but I got all muddled up. I think it is unfair that a Jamaican should be expected to sit for such a history paper three months after leaving Jamaica and pass it. I would have loved to get into grammar school but I had to go to this lousy secondary modern. I don't like it there. The teachers are stupid. I've wasted my time. I am doing my CSE next week. I don't think I'll stay to do GCE. I am leaving and doing a typing course instead.'

\*

*Black girl-pupil – doing GCEs at technical college:* 'Few black children get into grammar schools in Handsworth – I can only think of about three. Are black people so stupid that of the hundreds of kids in school in this dump you could count those in grammar schools on the fingers of one hand?'

\*

*Three black parents:* 'My Dave is quick on the uptake. He's always been a bright boy. The teacher he had before was very good and helped him on. This present teacher is not interested in the kids. She thinks of them and calls them "black little horrors". Some of them in the school are like that. So Dave is going down and down. I wish he were old enough to leave that school.'

'The school is overcrowded. The teachers have too many children in their classes and the children don't get enough attention. As long as they are in there they will never learn. I try to teach Janice at home myself.'

'The children like the school. I like the head teacher because I think he understands. But teachers come and go there too often. The kids never really have a chance to get used to them.'

\*

'In earlier years (1964 and 1965) when the average length of schooling was lower, it was indeed more difficult to obtain apprenticeships for immigrant school leavers, especially late arrivals. It is very likely, therefore, that there are a number of young people in their early twenties who are capable of more skilled work than that which they are doing. The problem is not confined to those of immigrant origin, but it is probable that the majority are from overseas ... it may be advisable to examine what can be done to increase opportunities for "a second chance" or training for every young adult, whether immigrant or not, who is willing to make the effort. Your sub-committee's detailed inquiries have shown that there is no evidence of serious unemployment and that many young people of immigrant origin find it possible to obtain posts offering systematic training, but that it is generally more difficult for them to do so than for young people born and brought up in Birmingham.' – *From a youth employment sub-committee report to Birmingham Education Committee, 2 March 1970.*

\*

*West Indian householder:* 'People talk about race relations in Britain being nothing like in America. If these fascist pigs were armed with guns, then people would realize just how like America this place really is. The way they don't think twice about pushing your face down the toilet bowl in the police station and denying it like hell afterwards, is the same way they wouldn't think twice about putting a bullet through your back. The fascist pigs remember well all they learnt at school, if some of them ever did go to school, about black people, and all that their parents taught them about black people. They don't meet us as human beings. They meet us as dogs, and we have got to treat them the same way.'

\*

*Policeman – asked to comment on complaints that police go to break up wedding receptions, parties, etc. without warrants:* 'You could go on from now till kingdom come, talking about police strong-arm measures, but I'll gladly give you the opportunity any day to get into this uniform and go and break up one of those shebeens or blues parties. When these people have their heads full of pot and alcohol, spurred on by the thumping beat of these reggae records, they are not humans any more, and only those who don't like themselves would set out to treat them as humans. You go there representing authority, you speak to them and you get no sense out of them. All you get is f—ing this and f—ing that, and they all begin to crowd around so there is really only one way to deal with them.'

\*

*West Indian householder who has lived in Birmingham for ten years:* 'Everyone in this establishment, and the police in particular, is out to make sure that they get the black man with his back up against the wall. You apply for a church hall to keep a blues party and the parochial church council rules that the hall is going to be wrecked and that the neighbours will be inconvenienced by all these drunken black men going home late at night. The education authorities wouldn't dream of letting you have a school hall. So you have your blues in your house, you apply for a bar licence which you know will not be granted. So you have your blues and sell your drinks, and before you know it Babylon cons his way in and unless you have enough guys in there to fight them back they confiscate your drinks, arrest you for selling alcohol without a licence, for violating fire precautions by having too many people in the building. If the guys are found smoking the stuff they charge you with allowing your premises to be used for smoking pot. So what do you do? At least the guys make sure that before anyone is arrested a few cops get well and truly knocked about. But then if they do arrest anyone after all that, they all take their revenge on the poor bloke from the moment he is put into the police car until he is perhaps taken to the hospital. And then, when they come next time, they come fifty men stronger.'

\*

*A police sergeant:* 'The black man seems to think he ought to be exempted from the authority of the law. He resents being approached by the police for any reason. West Indians in particular believe they know their rights more than everyone else. The number of ridiculous complaints made against the police is enough to make one not take these people seriously.'

\*

*Black mother of four children, two in their teens:* 'The police don't worry me and I don't worry them. I go to work, come home, watch TV and go to sleep. I keep my children around me. Heaven help them the day any one of them make a policeman come and knock my door. All those you say that complain about the police it is their own fault. They shouldn't find themselves in places where the police could get at them.'

\*

*Sir Wintringham Stable, a judge for thirty years, now retired:* 'I have not the slightest colour prejudice but I think England and Wales and Scotland are the homelands of their nationals. Of course we can absorb a certain number of strangers but it is absolutely impossible to absorb the vast numbers of immigrants we have let in. And the reason is that they do not want to be absorbed. What do people calling themselves multi-racialists really envisage in 100 years' time? A sort of hybrid race? It is a legitimate question to ask but one waits for the answer.' *Speech to Welshpool Conservative club, 6 September 1970.*

\*

*Mrs Elizabeth Relph, Church of England Children's Society:* 'Usually we find people are willing to adopt Asian or Oriental children, very willing to accept a tiny Asian girl, but Negroid children are much more difficult to place, especially boys past the baby stage.' *Quoted in the* Evening Standard *21 September 1970.*

*A white woman who adopted a black child:* 'Adopting a coloured child is something you want to say about life. It may grow up to be a Black Panther and to hate you; but if, like us, you really believe in the "melting pot" idea, then even that's worth risking.' *Quoted in the* Sunday Telegraph, *4 July 1970.*

\*

*Under the headline 'My Daily Embarrassment' the* Evening Standard *published the following letter on 17 February 1970:*

In these days of racial tension and strife, I should just like to record one particular incidence of a situation which embarrasses me daily in my work running an accountancy personnel selection organization. A young, highly intelligent and exceptionally well-qualified man from one of our former colonies applied to me recently for help in finding a job. After taking an Honours Law degree in London, he obtained three further degrees – Association of the Institute of Banking, Associate of the Chartered Institute of Secretaries and Associate of the Institute of Cost and Works Accountants. Were he not coloured, by now he would have been offered the pick of several dozen jobs paying £3,000 a year and more; however, as he is coloured, I have been unable to fix up even one interview for him. This occurs at a time when there is a vast shortage of young qualified accountants – in my experience about twenty jobs for every man, and if I cared I could report dozens of firms to the Race Relations Board. I do not choose to do so, but how long will we Britons pay lip service to the ideals of equality of opportunity while conducting a shameful campaign of prejudice against such men ? – *George D. Maxwell, G. D. Maxwell Associates, 29 Ludgate Hill, E.C.4.*

*

A Sikh religious leader died in London and to be buried in accordance with his faith his ashes – with the bones uncrushed – had to be put into running water. The body was cremated at Manor Park Crematorium, East London, and his followers sought local police permission to use the Thames. This was given, although a person's ashes may legally be scattered anywhere, so there was no need to ask. As the remains were being immersed at Runnymede a company director, Mr Malcolm Fordyce, came past in a motor boat. 'We were surprised, to say the least,' he told the *Daily Telegraph* (30 October 1970), 'and the children were a bit upset. It is hardly the thing you would expect to see in this country and I don't think it should be allowed.' Mr Fordyce informed the police, who launched a murder hunt. The religious leader's remains were brought up by police frogmen. Next day's newspapers talked of 'Ganges style funeral on Thames' but the police realized it was all a mistake and gave the dead man's remains back to the Sikhs to return to the water, which they did. From their extensive coverage of the matter the newspapers assumed public opinion would be shocked. The

Immigration Control Association said it was to protest to the Home Secretary and Minister of Health. One man at least spoke up for the Sikhs: in a letter to the *Daily Telegraph* (5 November 1970) Mr P. B. Dolphin of Gzira, Malta, said:

I was deeply shocked by your account (30 Oct) of the Asian funeral in the Thames and its aftermath. It seems that the mourners, now being hounded by the authorities, had scrupulously tried to observe the law by obtaining police permission before the ceremony. One wonders what crime they have committed, and what will now happen to the cremated bones which they obviously revere. The company director's report shows the ceremony to have been a simple and rather moving one. It is surprising that it caused so much indignation and such upset to his family, exposed as they must be to daily doses of television violence and brutality.

There will, of course, be none of the popular mass demonstration against this callous action. But it does deserve serious consideration, if only as a microcosm of society's reactions. So often the law turns a blind eye to mass anti-social behaviour (often politically manipulated) whereas in this case it is using a sledge hammer to crush a pathetically small nut. It is most tragic to see England making the worst of both worlds, by gaining notoriety through her permissiveness and at the same time deliberately forfeiting her once well earned reputation for tolerance. The situation is made the more poignant by the Indians' choice of Runnymede for their ceremony. Perhaps they believe that the spirit of Magna Carta still lives.

# 3. A black man in a white street

Hubert Thomas is an ordinary Jamaican. He cares passionately for his family, enjoys a glass of beer with his friends, and lives that rather narrow, selfish life common to all who like to keep out of trouble. Even so, Hubert unwittingly committed every mistake in the racist's book of hate and came near to receiving a stiff prison sentence which would have had disastrous results for his family. Buying a house in the white section of a street, marrying a white wife, and doing two jobs to get enough money to improve his living standards were Hubert's mistakes. Yet the five months of suffering he and his family endured in 1969 had been gestating for eleven years, some might say much longer – from the time the first European set eyes on black people in Africa.

In 1953 Hubert threw up his job as a plasterer in Jamaica and stowed away on a ship to Britain. He was caught, given three weeks imprisonment at Southampton, and deported to the West Indies. A year later he sailed in again as a legal immigrant determined to make for himself a better life than was possible in the Caribbean. He is a mongrel and not ashamed to say so. His family snapshot album shows that his father could pass for a white man because *his* father was a Chinese from Hong Kong and his mother was half Welsh and half Negro. On Hubert's mother's side his grandfather was a Scotsman called Forrester and his grandmother a Negro. Hubert's five brothers and sisters have various complexions and features but this he says 'has never stopped us from being a happy family'. Hubert is six feet tall, well-built, light copper in complexion and has features that are mixed Negro and Chinese. With so much British blood in his veins, and with Jamaica a British Crown colony from 1666 until independence within the Commonwealth in 1962, he considered himself as near British as makes no difference.

Like most immigrants, Hubert, once he had landed, drifted to the area where he had relatives. His brother lived in Moss Side, Manchester, a seedy, crumbling area of terraced houses soon to be swept away by a local authority redevelopment scheme. At first Hubert worked on the railway, then as a labourer in a rubber works and later had a spell as a carborundum process worker. Hubert hoisted himself out of this spell of dirty work, for which Britain needed immigrants desperately during the 'never had it so good' 1950s, to the next step up the ladder for the aspiring black man: driving a bus. This was more to his taste and he served Manchester's commuters well for six years. With overtime he could average £23 take-home pay most weeks. He courted and married a pretty Irish girl from the Curragh called Ita and after a spell in rented rooms, with a baby on the way, her father loaned them £150 for a deposit on a house.

For £750 they bought number 171 Russell Street, Moss Side – and accidentally took the first step on the road which, eleven years later, landed them in the middle of racial violence. Ita did the house-hunting while Hubert was at work. She spotted this little terraced home and liked it because it was near Alexandra Park, where the children might go and play. She inspected the premises, saw the agents, and put the deal through solicitors. Neither the agents nor the other residents of Russell Street caught a glimpse of Hubert. Whether Hubert's being in the background was by accident or design, the pair are now not very clear, with the passage of time, but it is common practice for mixed racial couples to employ this tactic.

But by ill-luck the Thomases bought into one of Moss Side's special roads. Two main roads cross Russell Street, splitting it into three parts which can easily be mistaken for three separate roads. The two northern sections have residents of various race but the southern section, where 171 lies, had always been wholly white. There are several all-white roads in Moss Side although they are hemmed in by multi-racial roads. They are kept all-white by the vendors and their neighbours insisting that the estate agents do not sell to blacks because they have the English-man's most dreaded fear of a decline in the value of his property

The homes in the southern section of Russell Street, where the Thomases moved to, are slightly better in quality. Many have bay windows and their owners obviously spend more on paint and repairs, and some have changed the solid wood doors to frosted glass to give a more modern, middle-class appearance. It is, of course, the end nearest to Alexandra Park and the furthest from the English version of a ghetto.

Moss Side has always been a tough area. Before the West Indians and the Pakistanis, there were the Irish, living rum-bustiously but on the whole peacefully alongside the native Mancunians. It has always had a high crime rate, been a place where the all-night drinker could go to a 'shebeen' just by hailing a taxi, and was famous for its prostitution. The trade flourishes mainly from clubs, pubs and private premises nowadays but still some street-walkers can be seen. Moss Side has always been the vice area at which the rest of Manchester could throw its respectable hands up in horror and many a municipal election candidate has ridden into the city council chamber on the backs of a 'clean up Moss Side' campaign. Once on the council, the campaign is forgotten. Unfortunately, at the time around the middle 1950s when black people began living in Moss Side, the drug cult was getting a hold on Britain. Inevitably, with its built-in network of racketeers, ponces and hustlers Moss Side became a centre of the illicit drug trade. The growth of the coloured population and the drug cult went in tandem, but to ascribe this entirely to black people, as the police are apt to, is a transparent injustice when the procession of white people passing through the courts on drugs offences is seen.

It was not long after the Thomases moved into Russell Street that the neighbours spotted Hubert and realized that he had penetrated the white barrier. Worse, he had a white wife, and those who cross the line and marry outside their own race are often regarded with greater hostility by poorly educated people. And perhaps as significant as the race factor was the fact that both Mr and Mrs Thomas are lapsed Roman Catholics – Hubert s an agnostic while Ita believes in God but does not attend church – for there are several first- and second-generation Irish families living in Russell Street. The family's early years in Moss Side were uneventful. The colour question in Britain had not yet come to the level of intense controversy it was to reach after Enoch Powell's 1968 speeches, and the racism, when it began to show, had to await the movement of the Thomases' children into the wider community. In the first years there would be an occasional snide remark to Ita as she went down the street past the pairs of gathering women such as 'Couldn't you have done better than marry a black man?' – the question always flung from behind when she was a few paces past the speaker. While there was never open racial confrontation these taunts kept the feeling always present in the background. On his way home from work Hubert would sometimes hear the statement 'he *is* a nigger' coming from groups of women who were trying to decipher his racial characteristics. It was when the children began to play in the street that the signs of tension became apparent. After four years in Russell Street came the first incident leading to blows. Hubert lost his temper when he believed a neighbour had hit one of his children. There were the usual summonses and cross-summonses for assault but it ended with handshakes in court.

Hubert and Ita had the feeling that the street was putting pressure on them through excessive fault-finding with their children. The two girls, Teresa and Anita, suffered badly from the crude sniping. Adults frequently told them: 'Your daddy's a nigger' and the abuse would sometimes be repeated by their own playmates when they argued and fell out at play. Frequently the girls ran home to their mother crying: 'We're not niggers, are we?' In fact, seeing the two girls in their trim, brown Whalley Range High School uniforms one would not easily guess their racial origins. Only a person racially conscious, or an investigator, would give them a second look as not being average English girls. The three boys, Tony, David and Alan, naturally got into scrapes in the street with a football striking a window pane or a saucy firework thrown into a backyard or under someone's feet. In April 1969 – when things were worst – Mr Thomas and Mr

Patrick Hickey, who lived further down the street, fought on th
pavement after Mr Hickey had chased one of the boys down th
street.

Some measure of the heightening tension could be seen in th
effect on David, then nine. He is very slightly darker than hi
brothers and sisters and whenever the subject of race came up
in the house he screamed: 'I'm white! I'm not black! I'm white!
He developed a speech defect around this time and had to under
go therapy. His mother has had two serious nervous breakdown
in recent years, requiring hospital treatment, and she is often
heavily dosed with Librium by her doctor to keep her calm
During the warm summer days of July and August that year th
storm was gathering for the Thomases. Racial conflict through
out Britain had increased considerably, erupting on 27 July in
Leeds with the worst race riots so far seen in Britain (see Chapter
fourteen).

In Moss Side the police had upset the blacks by making a
drive on illicit drug users and using their powers under the Dan
gerous Drugs Act, 1965, to stop and search people in the street
or at house parties. Black people felt that they were being un
fairly singled out for these searches and some retaliated, leading
to charges of assault on the police. Several blue-beat parties
where drinks were sold illegally were raided that summer as the
West Indians danced and drank the Saturday nights away.

In June an incident occurred which confirmed the worst fears
of the black community. As the Manchester correspondent of
*The Times* later reported (7 November 1970):

A police sergeant carried out a 'serious assault' on a West Indian,
took him to a police station and charged him with an offence he had
not committed. Judge Derek Hodgson decided this at the Salford
Hundred Court of Record in Manchester yesterday when he ordered
the sergeant and the chief constable of Manchester to pay £500
damages. Mr Newton Wilson Walker, aged 46, a labourer of Raby
Street, Moss Side, Manchester, had sued Sergeant Lachlan McPherson
Carver and the Chief Constable, Mr William James Richards, for
damages for assault, false imprisonment, malicious prosecution and
trespass.

The judge [according to the *Times* report] said he was satisfied that the first three complaints had been made out but dismissed the allegation of trespass. In his reserved judgment the judge said: 'I think the first defendant lost his temper and did strike the plaintiff. Mr Walker had earlier told the court that he parked his car in Greame Street, Moss Side, at 5.15 a.m. in June last year to call for a friend. He alleged that Sergeant Carver started to question him and when he tried to get out of the car the officer slapped, punched and kicked him. He said he was put in a police van, taken to Platt Lane police station, and charged with using threatening words of behaviour likely to cause a breach of the peace. He was found Not Guilty of that charge at the city magistrates' court. His allegation that while he was in custody police had moved his car without permission was rejected by the judge.

'I believe that the first defendant came to the conclusion that he had caught or was likely to have caught a car stealer,' the judge said. 'The hour of the morning, the district and perhaps the colour of the plaintiff's skin led him to those conclusions although they were unjustified and unreasonable. I think that the sergeant, in temper, when his actions were being witnessed, threw the plaintiff violently against the side of the car. I regret to say that I do not think the defendant would have behaved in this way if he had known he was being watched. And while I am not prepared to hold that the defendant was kicking the plaintiff hard, he may well have been nudging him with his boot to get a by now terrified man to his feet.'

That summer the noisy, gay parties, with reggae, the new sound, bouncing out of the windows and over the roofs, became infamous all over Britain. It was partly the weather, partly the intolerance of the whites, partly the 'up you' attitude now prevalent among the harassed blacks. Militant black organizations found themselves with a larger, keener membership and new groups sprouted. There is no evidence that Hubert Thomas ever had any dealings with Black Power organizations, but, inevitably, their paths were joining.

As the summer holidays began at the end of July the level of children's games in the street naturally increased. There are no gardens for the householders to retire to, and nobody wants to sit in a backyard along with the dustbins and outside toilet. Sunning is done on the pavement if you do not feel like walking to the park. The children played around the alleys through the terraced houses and along the pavement. In a couple of weeks the nerves of the parents and other adults were getting somewhat tattered and increasingly the children disputed among themselves. A holiday would have helped. Although Hubert was at the time a machine operator in a Trafford Park factory, working the night shift, coming home to sleep in the mornings, and decorating houses in the afternoon and early evening, his money did not run to giving the family a change of scenery. The niggling things which happened in the street that summer led Hubert and Ita to conclude that at least two thirds of the street were against them and subsequent events tend to prove this.

About 4 p.m. on Thursday, 7 August, the Thomas boys had a quarrel with their playmates in the street and blows were exchanged. All the youngsters ran home and proclaimed, quite naturally, to their parents: 'It wasn't me.' It could have died down but a woman knocked at the Thomases' front door and said: 'Two of your boys have belted my son. It's not fair'. Ita promised to rebuke her boys, said she was sorry, and closed the door. But soon she heard it was not her sons' fault and started up the street to put over her point of view.

'Mind your own business! Get down your own end!' were the shouts she got as she approached three women up the street to give them a piece of her mind. The irate Mrs Thomas shouted back and a fight started between her and the three women. 'They held me up against the wall and belted my face,' says Ita. 'There were four on to me.' She shouted to one of the children to get their father and Hubert raced up and struck two of the women. The fighting, screaming and shouting was just dying down as the police came. They advised the conflicting parties to take out cross-summonses and drove away. This fracas was really no more than the typical and frequent quarrels in a tough district. But the two fights that day were to be followed by two worse ones within twenty-four hours.

When Hubert reached home from decorating work at 7 p.m. the next day he learned that his boys had had a row with the Mr Hickey with whom he had fought earlier in the year. He told his wife he did not intend to fight Mr Hickey again but would take the two elder boys to the houses to clear things up. If the boys were wrong, he would make them apologize. But as Hubert approached Mr Hickey jumped up from his doorstep where he was sitting in the evening sunshine and struck Hubert. Mr Hickey later told a court:

I could see by the look on his face that he was going to hit me. It is correct I hit him first. On the 8th of April (the previous fight) I did not hit him first, he did all the hitting. On the 8th of August I could not afford to let the same thing happen again. I have four children. There is not a lot of trouble in the street with the children. I cannot say whether there has been trouble with the children – I keep myself to myself. The first trouble was about children. I do not know what the second trouble was about. The second occasion was just a rough and tumble between us.

It was in reality a fierce clash between two angry men. Like a fight in a cowboy film, they rolled over and over across the street in front of a big crowd which had rapidly gathered. Hubert claims that every time he got on top of his opponent, other men pushed him over and Mr Hickey got astride. Ita raced up with a poker grabbed from the hearth and began trying to beat Mr Hickey off her husband. Another woman grabbed it from her before she could do serious harm. Police came along in the Panda cars, broke up the fight and again advised private summonses, helping the quarrellers to exchange names and addresses so that the proceedings could be started.

The people went back into their homes and while things looked outwardly calm, the tension in and around Russell Street was mounting dangerously. If ever there was a time when an experienced community relations worker was needed on the scene to damp things down, this was it. But, although Manchester had one such officer – Mr Surendra Kumar, an Indian, with three white assistants – no one told them of the trouble. The police did not consider it their job to inform any of the race relations agencies or any social worker. But news of Hubert's humiliation flew around Moss Side. On a warm, lazy Sunday evening, with the cafés and bars full, gossip travels fast. Someone – it remains disputable who – went to a café in Great Western Street and related the events in Russell Street to a group of militants. Some of these men had recently had clashes with the police and were in an ugly mood. A few belonged to the West Indian United Association, a three-year old organization 'formed to protect and advance the interests of West Indian people, particularly in Manchester'. Two weeks before, this group temporarily aligned itself with the Universal Coloured People's Association's newly-formed Manchester branch, and, calling themselves the 'Black People's Self-Defence Front', had marched on Platt Lane police station as a protest against alleged police brutality. The protesters stamped around the station yard with banners declaring 'Moss Side bleeds in agony' and 'Stop police brutality'. Police did not intervene and the 100 protesters went away having made their point and got their picture in next day's issue of the *Guardian*. Hubert's eleven years of private torture by prejudice, and the current anger of the young militants, were beginning to fuse.

The fourth and final conflict came at 10 p.m. on that hot Friday night in August, just three hours after the clash with Mr Hickey. The incident was brief, violent and sinister. There was a knock at Hubert's door and he found two well-dressed coloured men on the step who said they were from the Race Relations Board. They had heard, they said, that Hubert was suffering from discrimination and had been treated violently. Would Hubert mind pointing out to them at which houses the people lived? Hubert believed them and, with his elder daughter Teresa to help, started up the street with the two 'officials' and began pointing out the houses of four people involved in the fights. Suddenly, as they did so, about fourteen blacks jumped out of a side alley and started smashing windows with bricks and sticks. Hubert and Teresa fled. One white householder, Mr Arthur Scullion, fought the gang and then retreated. But his wife, who was returning to her home with some beer, was struck as she was coming down the road and had to have hospital treatment for an injured shoulder. Windows in three houses were broken. This time the police came with dogs but, once again, the worst was over by the time they arrived.

Hubert was terrified at the way things had snowballed and

hid at his brother's house in Brooks Bar for the weekend. The race fight was reported in the next day's *Manchester Evening News* and referred to a black man wielding an iron bar whom the police wanted to interview. Friends told Hubert that he was the man the police were looking for. By Monday, Hubert, still in hiding, frightened and bewildered, sent a message to Mr Roy White, the Jamaican High Commissioner's representative in Manchester asking for advice and help. Mr White replied that he must see the police but, to quiet Hubert's fears caused by the stories of police ill-treatment, advised that before he did so he must be examined by a doctor to ascertain his exact physical condition. Hubert's face was in fact still bruised from the fight with Mr Hickey.

Mr White took Hubert to Platt Lane police station by car and remained with him throughout the interview. Hubert gave the detectives a disjointed account of his life in Russell Street and related how the 'men from the Race Relations Board' had hoaxed him. Detective Sergeant Raymond Sherratt told Hubert:

I think your story is as untruthful as it is incredible. You virtually admit that you have grievances against the people in your street and you tell me that you took a crowd of men down and pointed out houses in order that they should take details and report them to some organization or other and further more that you did not expect violence. I do not believe you.

At which stage (the record shows) Hubert protested: 'I never, I never do any of these things.' Detective Sergeant Sherratt told Hubert that he was satisfied that he deliberately took a gang of coloured men into Russell Street with the intention of causing trouble and that he struck Mrs Scullion. So Hubert was charged with causing grievous bodily harm with intent, an offence which on conviction carries a maximum of three years' imprisonment.

The outcome of Hubert's call at the police station was bitterly ironic, even supposing he was guilty. Of all those, black and white, involved in the mêlées he was the only one charged with any offence. True he had lost his temper on occasions, he had been present at the final conflict, but most reasonable people would say that at the very worst he was as much sinned against as sinning. The news that he alone had been charged flew around Moss Side and the racial climate deteriorated further but fortunately there were no further incidents. The militant black organizations talked a lot in the next few months about the injustice of Hubert's being singled out for prosecution, and used it in their campaigns against the police. The police considered they had done a proper day's work: there had been an incident; a woman was hurt; a man was charged; the justice of their action was up to the court. The psychological and racial complications were not their business, an attitude they may soon have to adjust if they are to keep pace with the changing social climate in Britain. Country folk have a saying: 'It's a Bobby's job', meaning an easy task. It used to be an easy task being a British policeman, not necessarily because we have the best police force but because we were the most law-abiding people in the world. And a policeman's duties used not to encounter sensitive areas like politics, race and student protest. Now it does and the policeman is complaining. We read of twenty more policemen being added to Scotland Yard's illegal immigration and drugs department but not of their hiring any social psychologists or psychiatrists to keep them abreast of the times. Until the police see their role as partly therapeutic and not only as crime-busters, the decline in police–public harmony will continue.

Hubert was given bail because of his good character and waited three months for his trial. His solicitor, Mr Jeffrey Wilner, decided that they could not bring in the previous fights or the racial prejudice as a defence because this could be taken to show that Hubert had good reason to hit Mrs Scullion. When the case was reached at Manchester Crown Court the prosecution produced seven neighbours as witnesses, while Hubert had only himself and one witness – his thirteen year-old daughter Teresa. The case seemed so strong against Hubert that plea-bargaining began before the trial, in which one of the authors of this book became involved, incredibly and quite wrongly in his view. At the last moment, when Hubert was actually in the dock, the prosecution came forward with the suggestion that they would not press the charge of grievous bodily harm with intent, with its three-year jail maximum, if Hubert would plead guilty to making an affray, which would probably get him six months. Hubert did not know what to do. He was terrified at the prospect of a long jail sentence as he knew his wife's health was not strong enough to hold the family together, and the children might have to go into local authority care. Mr Leslie Portnoy, the defence barrister, said it was not ethical for him to advise which course to take. The huge court was almost empty except for the judge, waiting to know whether it was going to be a long trial or a brief 'up and down' one, and as Hubert looked around for help in his decision the only face he knew was a journalist whom he had met just after the incident which led to the charge.

Hubert asked me (writes Derek Humphry) to come over to the dock. Mr Portnoy explained the position and Hubert asked 'What shall I do?' I felt it was not my position to tell him how to take such an important decision so quickly and looked around for his family or friends, the proper people from whom Hubert should take advice. There were none. It was the most difficult question ever put to me in twenty-five years as a journalist, and my mouth went dry with apprehension as Hubert, by now desperate, appealed for a decision. The judge tapped his pencil restlessly – he must have thought it odd that the prisoner was having a conference with a reporter – and to gain time for the three of us to think I talked emptily about the various penalties and the weight of evidence, when, quite suddenly Hubert blurted out: 'Well, I didn't hit the woman; and if I didn't I don't see why I should go to prison.' The directness and honesty of the remark so impressed Mr Portnoy that he swivelled instantly from the prisoner to face the Judge and rapped out: 'My client pleads not guilty, my Lord.' It was a snap action with which I agreed, partly through relief that Hubert had taken his own decision. But as the prosecution case began I began to have my doubts as to its wisdom.

In his opening remarks the prosecutor referred to 'a horrible street brawl' in which 'rightly or wrongly there was some colour prejudice.' It set the stage for a trial which was saturated with the race issue. The first witness was the injured woman, Mrs Margaret Scullion, who said that as she came up to her doorway she saw four coloured men in the road with Mr Thomas near her doorstep:

The four coloured men were running around in the middle of the road shouting and throwing bottles and bricks. I said to Mr Thomas, 'Go away and leave us alone.' I threw the can of beer at him as a reaction. It missed. He started swinging a stick and struck me several blows and when I fell down I was hit again on the shoulder. Police sirens started and he ran away.

In cross-examination she remarked that 'there are no other coloured people in that part of the road' and that 'we do not regard him as coloured', which contrasted strangely with the statement later that she saw five coloured people fighting with her husband whereas earlier she had said four plus Mr Thomas. Her husband then described his fight at the front door with Mr Thomas and three others. 'They were black', he said starkly. Mr Scullion said: 'I didn't know he [Hubert] was living in the street until that night' although he had owned a house in the road for eighteen months.

Gossiping about the affair in pubs and cafés before the trial, the black militants who had taken part had said that they went to Russell Street to help Hubert after hearing of the three fights but when they arrived a trap was waiting for them. The white residents, they said, came out of their houses and took them on. An indication that this might be true came from another witness for the prosecution Mr Frederick Cawley, a baker. He told the jury:

I heard a banging on the wall from Mr Scullion next door. It was a signal for me to phone the police. Then a brick came through the window of the hall door. It was a prearranged signal arranged after the first incident if there was trouble. I expected trouble coming back.

The injured woman's mother, Mrs Frances Reilly, who lived a few doors away, described how 'on a very warm night' she saw Hubert come out of the alley with about eight or nine 'coloured fellows' behind him. 'I have never classed Mr Thomas as a coloured man; the others were real coloured men,' she said, alleging that Hubert had called for 'one through here', whereupon 'a darkie threw a brick through Mr Cawley's window'. She told the court that although she knew Hubert she had nothing to do with him. 'I don't class Mr Thomas as a darkie: his children are as white as mine.' While all the seven neighbours said Hubert was present and had a stick, only the injured woman actually said he struck the blows involved in the charge. It was, perhaps, all summed up by the evidence of Mrs Marjorie Rose:

> I heard the noise and came out and saw Mr Thomas, *whom I knew*, with six or seven coloured people. *They* were in Mrs Scullion's doorway hitting her. She was against the wall. Mr Thomas was at the bottom of the steps. I couldn't say who was hitting. They had sticks or bars. When the police came they ran away.

Clearly Hubert was in the dock because he was the only black face to which the neighbours could put a name. The prosecution plugged away at the witness's constant references to Hubert having pointed something out, in their view the houses which were to be smashed. In the event, the whole case turned on whether or not Hubert believed they were from the Race Relations Board.

During his evidence lasting 110 minutes Hubert was remarkably consistent in his story, which he had told to the police at Platt Lane, and repeated to me on two occasions. Yet the prosecution asserted that he had gone to the cafe in Great Western Street and brought the gang down to cause trouble. Hubert's reply to this was: 'There are militant groups of people in Moss Side who will take these actions. They must have heard about the earlier incident.' The prosecution were unable to call any evidence to support their theory of Hubert calling in retaliators. His story to the jury was this:

> I was sitting inside with my little girl Teresa when two coloured gentlemen came to my door. I had never met them before. I did not ask them their names. They said they had heard that coloured people were being beaten up by white people and they would like to investigate. They said they were from the Race Relations Board and looked like officials, well-spoken and well-dressed. I went back into the

house to get Teresa so she could help me point out the houses. As Teresa pointed out who lived in the houses I would say 'That's one and that's one.' Just as she pointed to one house a group of coloured men – about nine or twelve – came running out of an alley and started throwing bricks. I had nothing in my hand and ran away immediately. I was frightened.

The complexities of race labelling were curiously raised during Hubert's evidence. He strenuously denied that he used the term 'coloured' in his statement to the police. He declared: 'I have always regarded people as people; I don't use the word "coloured".' But in fact he does use the word, in conversation; this was his attempt at keeping the race issue out of the trial.

Even under close cross-examination, Hubert's only witness, little Teresa, backed her father's story in every detail. The reason she had to take her father and the men from the 'Race Relations Board' up the road was that her father didn't know at which houses the Scullions or the Hickeys lived. The prosecutor told the Judge that Hubert 'must be utterly stupid' if he went into the street where he had been the victim of violence to point out the houses and to take his daughter with him. 'So concerned is he with racial harmony that he has done nothing about it; so concerned that he has made no complaint to the Race Relations Board,' said the prosecutor. In his closing speech, the defending counsel, Mr Portnoy, reminded the jury that

prejudice can creep in so insidiously. Common sense tells you that there is going to be ill feeling in this street which is all white. You may be a bit embarrassed to hear about English men and women behaving in this way.

The prosecution had made much of Teresa's being taken to the incident. 'Did this man take his daughter to a riot?' asked Mr Portnoy. 'The worst criminal wouldn't take his daughter to a riot, and this was at least a mini-riot.' It was, he said, the easiest thing in retrospect to transfer Hubert's face on to the assailant, particularly when there had been ill feeling in the street.

Judge Bailey asked the jury to keep the colour issue 'in the background'. He told them: 'The trouble in that street was to do with colour but don't let it affect your decision.' After the summing up of the evidence the jury went out, to return with their verdict within only thirteen minutes. Most lawyers say that a quick decision is usually a guilty verdict and those of us who felt sympathy with Hubert – and by now observers from the Community Relations Commission and the Jamaican High Commission were present – took our seats again with foreboding. The foreman announced the jury's verdict: Not guilty. The Judge seemed very surprised because he queried: 'Not guilty on any charge?' although there was only one charge on the books.

Hubert walked away from the court building, with his wife and children round him, a happy if bewildered man. They took a bus back to Moss Side to talk over whether they should continue to live in Russell Street. Hubert had often thought of emigrating to Canada but his wife was not keen. Perhaps the most tragic thing about Hubert is that the years of provocation have made him consider himself a second-class citizen. Discussing buying another house he remarked: 'When I decide which house I want I shall knock on a few doors and ask the neighbours if they mind my coming to live there.'

# 4. It takes a death to convince

Tausir Ali worked in a Wimpy Bar in the West End of London. It was a menial job but he lived carefully and was able to send money home regularly to his wife and children in Pakistan. On 6 April 1970 he left work just before midnight and caught a train to Bromley, got off, and began to walk to his flat in St Leonard's Road, Bow. Two eighteen-year-old white youths were on the same train but as they did not have tickets they jumped over a wall to escape the collector and landed close to Mr Ali. Between the railway bridge and the block of flats for which Mr Ali was heading they met, and they accompanied him to the block. On a stairway he received a severe knife wound to the throat. The youths ran away and Mr Ali staggered to the doorway of his flat and collapsed. Two hours later he died in hospital. The youths later claimed Mr Ali had invited them home, implying that it was for some immoral purpose, but there was no evidence of Mr Ali being a homosexual. At the Central Criminal Court the prosecuting counsel said it was right for the jury to bear in mind that some young men went in for the pastime known as 'Paki-bashing'. One youth pleaded not guilty to murder but guilty to manslaughter on the grounds of diminished responsibility.

His plea was accepted and he was sent to a mental institution 'without limit to time' after a doctor had said that he was mentally abnormal and in need of treatment. The second youth was acquitted on the judge's direction.

While the trial of Tausir Ali's killer attracted little attention, his death was perhaps the most significant happening in the history of Pakistani settlement in Britain. For two years the Pakistani community in London had been insisting that they were being attacked in the streets on a scale which exceeded normal street crime rates. The politicians, the police and the press ignored their cries, arguing that there was always a certain amount of 'mugging' on the streets of the Metropolis but no one was picking on the Pakistanis in particular. It did not help their case that many of the attacks were not reported to the police. This is largely explained by the poor English spoken by so many Pakistanis, and their shyness, even dread, of the police stations. And how many white Englishmen after an incident say 'what's the use?' when they haven't a clear idea of who robbed them or want to avoid further bother?

There had been more than forty attacks on Pakistanis in the East End alone in the six months before Mr Ali died. Granada Television's World in Action programme investigated their plight in depth, and revealed some hair-raising features of racism in the area. 'The Pakistanis make me crawl,' said one woman. The programme went virtually unnoticed (although it was to be shown again privately to race relations agencies *after* the controversy), but one piece of news suddenly caught attention. The staff at the London Chest Hospital, one third of whom are black, drew up a petition asking for maximum protection after two of their colleagues had been attacked by skinheads. The Sinhalese registrar in cardiology was attacked only a few yards from the hospital by skinheads who broke his nose. He escaped and ran into the hospital. The Pakistani night telephonist was assaulted at Bethnal Green tube station as he went to buy a ticket. 'Here comes old Harry Krishna,' said one youth and a gang of crop-haired youths with 'bovver' boots kicked him in the face and stomach. He was in hospital for four days and treatment for a damaged eye continued for many weeks.

Suddenly Paki-bashing was news and the police added extra night patrols to guard the 5,000 Asians in the borough of Tower Hamlets. A bureau was set up by community relations officer Joe Hunte so that Pakistanis could take their complaints for a sympathetic hearing. The news media were now convinced of the seriousness of the situation but the police, the Home Office and the Community Relations Commission apparently were not. The police argued that there had not been as many attacks as claimed

by the Pakistani community and would not accept that peopl
who had been attacked and not gone straight to a police statio
had anything to complain about later. One fear the Pakistan
had – it was also the high season for illegal immigration stories i
the press – was of being detained as possible illegal immigrants
they went near a police station. True or false, there were account
circulating in the East End at the time among the Asians of the
colleagues who had spent one or two days 'inside' while the
right to be in the country was checked by the authorities.

The attacks were not only personal. Hashim Ullah's grocer
shop looks at night like a blacked-out fortress awaiting attack
On either side the shops are gaily lit so passers-by can do a littl
window-shopping. By contrast, Mr Ullah's large windows ar
heavily shuttered and the fanlights are carefully covered wit
chicken wire. So as a food shop its appearance is not very in
viting. But there are good reasons why his shop in the East En
of London is well barricaded – eight times in the past fiv
months the windows have been shattered at night. Each time h
rushes to the window of his flat above the shop and sees teenag
gangs rushing away. The neighbouring shops, owned by whit
people for white customers, are untouched. Mr Ullah is Pakistan
and caters mainly for Pakistanis, and he draws the obvious con
clusion. Mr Ullah's harassment is typical of many Pakistan
shopkeepers throughout inner London who are obliged to fortif
their premises because the insurance companies have long sinc
stopped paying out to replace plate glass.

The Pakistani groups talked of forming 'vigilante' patrols t
roam the streets at night to protect their fellow countrymen an
women from the skinheads, but this brought universal condemna
tion from the government, the police and the church. The 'vig
lante' desire sprang mainly from the extreme left wing group
like the Pakistan Workers' Union. The more moderate Pakista
Welfare Association and the National Federation of Pakistan
Associations, while insisting that they as a racial minority wer
being singled out for vicious attacks, stressed that it was th
duty of the police to increase protection.

It took Tausir Ali's death for Pakistanis to prove the point that their lives really were in danger. Because the two youths escaped unseen (and were not arrested for three weeks) the police hinted that it could have been a fight between two Pakistanis for all anyone knew. But the Pakistanis knew it was not one of themselves who had killed Tausir Ali and had no hesitation in denouncing it as another skinhead attack. The Pakistanis called a mass meeting in a bingo hall in the Commercial Road and opened it with a minute's silence in his memory. 'He was brutally murdered by local hooligans,' said Mr Abdur Raquid, general secretary of the Pakistani Federation. As there was no evidence at that time as to who killed Tausir Ali, the government and the police said nothing. The meeting passed a resolution 'demanding immediate and adequate measures to protect the life and the property of the law-abiding and peace-loving Pakistanis', of which the police took no notice because they argued that they endeavoured to protect everybody. "The police here are not concerned whether a man is black or white or where he was born,' the divisional police chief, Commander Maggs, told the rally of frightened Pakistanis, 'You are all treated equally.' He defended the police position by pointing out that many complainants could not identify their attackers, and as there were ten million people in London an assailant could lose himself on the other side of the capital within half an hour. 'Hooliganism and damage to property is on the increase in Britain,' stated Commander Maggs. 'For every one attack against a Pakistani there are many more against white people.'

Next day the Pakistan workers' union called a similar meeting and voted to form self-defence groups despite an appeal not to do so by Bishop Trevor Huddleston, the world-renowned opponent of apartheid and racism, in whose diocese of Stepney all the trouble had occurred. The militants collected forty names of volunteers for patrols but Mr Abul Ishaque, PWU secretary, said: 'We are giving the police a chance to put their house in order and if there is no more trouble then vigilante groups will not be necessary.' A similar threat for the same reasons had been

made in the Euston area two years before; the police there added
extra patrols, the vigilantes kept off the streets, and the attacks
died down. History repeated itself in the East End. The Community Relations Commission – the agency set up by Parliament
in 1968 to promote racial harmony, and in 1969 spending
£300,000 – floundered helplessly, not knowing how to ameliorate
the 'Paki-bashing' situation. 'Big Joe' Hunte, its local representative, strove courageously to cope without head office help. This
situation demonstrated again the need for a 'flying squad' of
race experts to move instantly into areas of sudden racial conflict.

Both moderate and militant Pakistani groups held marches
through London in the next few weeks in support of their cause
and both took angry letters to Harold Wilson at 10 Downing
Street calling for action. Their fellow countrymen from all
parts of Britain travelled to London to march in support.

There were also attacks on Asians in Luton and Wolverhampton during May 1970, but not, however, on the scale of the
East End assaults. Why are the Pakistanis in Britain given a
rougher time than any other immigrant group? A Pakistani is
small in stature, easy meat for a bully. He is calm and placid in
nature – until aroused. His race is easily identifiable by his pigmentation – ranging from swarthy to a striking smokey hue – and
sleek black hair with a good hairline. If he manages to master
the English language – no mean feat for an Asian – he speaks it
with such speed and accent that he is not easily understood. Many
are illiterate in their own tongue. He is a Pakistani because he is a
Muslim (the nation was separated from India for religious reasons); therefore his religion and his patriotism are one and the
same. His views of life and his culture spring from his ancient
religion, making it difficult to accommodate modern European
thinking. He probably comes from peasant stock and probably
knows Pakistan's cities even less than he knows ours. If he ever
gets his wife and children to Britain he is a lucky man; usually he
is stuck with a long period of celibacy and family separation. He
is poor not only because his job is likely to be unskilled and
ill-paid but because he is sending at least half his earnings home.

(Between £40 and £50 million a year leaves Britain from the Pakistani community.)

It is all too easy to look down upon a man who faces all these difficulties. To the narrow-minded and the bigot he is a man from another world. His contribution to the British economy goes unsung: he mans the night shifts in the cotton and woollen mills (while the few whites still in the industry are on the day shift); he sweats in the carbon black works of Smethwick and Southall and the foundries of the Black Country. He is cooking food, waiting on tables or cleaning up in the restaurants – especially in those run by British Rail – and generally working in the evenings when most prefer to be at home with the television set on. He's thrifty and acquisitive – his ancestors have fostered commerce all over the world – which make him a target for jealousy. He's the first to have his windows smashed if some hooligan wants to work off his feelings against blacks – and gets little sympathy when he complains. A stranger in a strange land. Go back? To live on £30 a year – if he's lucky enough to get a job! He is, after all, human.

Certain sections of the British public and press have treated him like dirt for years. The apocryphal story of the three Pakistanis who all wore the same pair of Tuf shoes for their eight-hour shifts and received a free pair under the six-month guarantee appeared in the *Daily Express* and other papers in the early 1960s. Since 1961 the yarn of the Pakistanis in the loft has circulated unabated, if a little varied. Back in 1961 the version went that the wife of a Vauxhall car worker in Luton working night shifts complained to her husband that she could hear noises in the roof when she was in bed. He stayed home one night and climbed through the trap door. He found a Pakistani sleeping between every joist in the loft of eight houses, which, being terraced, were linked through their one roof. This story can still be heard retailed as truth in towns all over Britain. ('I heard it from someone who knew.') But nobody has ever found an actual case of multi-occupation of a loft.

The Pakistanis have become a folk ogre through stories about swindling the social security, their beds never being cold and that most of them sneaked into the country in the night. Quite a few do live in overcrowded houses, for obvious reasons: some have entered the country illicitly, and the racketeers, black and white, who have organized this form of entry may find they have a heavier debt to pay to society for the image they are helping the Pakistanis to acquire than any court of law can levy.

# 5. The black Welshman who wanted to act

*In a few instances in this book we have felt it necessary to disguise*
*the names of the people involved to save them further hardship.*
*In others the people were happy to have their names used and in*
*some the names are already public knowledge, having appeared in*
*newspapers. In this chapter we make no apology for 'plugging'*
*the name of George Baizley, an actor who, because he is black,*
*has had an extraordinary struggle trying to 'make it'. This is his*
*story:*

I was born in Port Talbot, the eldest of four children. My father
came from Ghana out of curiosity around 1935. He stowed away.
He earned a living as a boxer but a split chin stopped him fighting
and he went to sea. Around thirty he met my mother; her father
was Portuguese and her mother Welsh. She also had Irish
ancestry. When I was a year old the family moved to Brixton in
London. My mother had always wanted to go on the stage but
couldn't afford it and she was keen on helping me. I went to tap-
dancing lessons and occasionally got film-extra work. There
weren't many blacks around at that time and a car would come
and take you to the studios. At six I appeared in *Men of Two*
*Worlds* in which Eric Portman was the star. I was part of the crowd
and wore a long African smock, and had to parade around some
mud huts. When I was about seven or eight I was an extra in
*The Huggetts Abroad* which starred Petula Clark. One day while
the filming was on I decided to appear solo in front of the
cameras and strolled across the scene when the film was on. I
was dragged off the set. I don't know why I did it; one of these
boyish things.

My dad made a living for a short time as a singer and appeared in the chorus of *Showboat* when it opened in London. Then he worked as a mechanic. I had another extra part in *Saraband of the Dead Lovers* when I was nine, and got £4 a day. This was a big help to the family budget because my father wasn't working then; he was having a hard time getting a job being coloured. I went to Hackford Road secondary modern school in Brixton but I hated it. I didn't like school because it stopped me from growing up and I wanted to grow up fast.

I didn't know what I wanted to do when I left school. I'd no desire to be an actor; it never crossed my mind. I took up a tailoring apprenticeship with a firm in the West End at £1 10s. a week but I quit after six months. It was not adventurous enough for me. I worked for a hairdressing supply firm for two weeks at £2 10s. and then one day a man came up to me in the street and asked if I was interested in a job in a plastics factory. It was a small family concern and it paid £3 10s. a week and you learned the trade of plastic moulding. When I got there I found a Turkish guy covered in soap; the conditions were pretty bad but I stayed there a year. I had to push raw materials into a kind of mould which produced shop dummies.

The gang I went around with at Brixton started going to an evening institute ran by the council. We didn't try to learn anything; we just mucked about. Then the principal hauled us in and said we either attended two classes or left. I asked what there was to learn and someone said acting. I said I'd try it for a laugh. A teacher called Terry took the class. The first thing he wanted us to do was just to come into the classroom and sit down on a chair with the other pupils watching. Terry said that out of twenty who did it I was the only one who did it a different way. I'd used my imagination, he said. Everybody else just walked in, sat down, and crossed their legs. I came in, turned the chair round, and sat on it with my legs between the back rest and my arms draped over. Terry asked me if I'd ever thought of taking up acting. I just laughed. I was sixteen. I tried to take the classes seriously but my mates said that Terry was just an old woman. So we larked around and got thrown out at the next lesson. But every time Terry met me in the street he would remind me about acting. He was trying to brainwash me. A bit later I told my pals that I would like to be an actor. They laughed and said prove it. They challenged me to walk across the street in full view of everybody and pretend to post an imaginary letter. They roared with laughter when I did.

But I didn't do anything about my ambition. I suppose it was because I didn't know what to do. It was around the time that immigrants were coming to Brixton at a rapid rate and I was shattered one day when my best friend, a white boy, suddenly said: 'In a year's time you'll be taken for an immigrant and they won't like you.' This was one of the most painful things ever said to me; not that my friend meant to hurt me; he was telling the truth as he saw it and I knew he was right.

I decided to chuck up the job in the plastics factory. The foreman asked me why and I told him I didn't want to be one of those people who worked all week and rushed down to the coast at the week-end. I felt there was something more to life than that. He told me 'you'll probably have to be one of those millions' but I got my cards and left. For a while I hung around the West End mixing with drug addicts and gamblers. The £12 I'd saved vanished in two days. One day a Salvation Army guy came over and said 'If you ever need help come and see us.' It always puzzled me why he picked me out and came over. I appreciated it.

I got into a fight and was knocked down. I was only slightly hurt and I thought, well, this isn't really the life for me. My nerves were bad and my mother was worried about me. My father got me a job as a receptionist in a night club. It was the first strip club in London – in Irving Street – and I stood at the door and checked the membership cards. I earned £1 a day, and with tips this came to £7 or £8 a week. But it was long hours: 2 p.m. to midnight, but at least it kept me across the water away from Brixton. I started gambling on horses and won some money and then I decided I'd fulfil a desire I'd always had to see Denmark. I'd been told that coloured artists really went down well in Denmark so I went over to stay with a friend. I got two engagements to sing in a big night club through some friends. I was supposed to sing 'Venus Draw Back Your Bow'. There were no rehearsals. When I got on the stage and the music started my mouth opened and my hands moved as though I was singing but no sound came out. The music master had just told the audience I was a big cabaret star from England and he was very angry. Stage fright had completely robbed me of my voice. I was taken off. The audience didn't go for me because they thought the microphone had broken down!

After six weeks in Denmark I didn't get another engagement and came back. I'd only been back four days when the phone rang and I was asked to do a Lux toilet soap advertisement for Nigeria cinema. I was two days in front of the camera and I realized then that I could act in front of a camera. I bought the *Stage* and looked through all the ads for drama schools. I saw the Actor's Workshop gave evening classes. I rang up and they said it cost £30 for a five-month term, so I got a labouring job at Schweppes in Vauxhall working from eight in the morning until ten at night. In three weeks I had enough to enrol at the Workshop.

It was a momentous step forward. Life in Brixton was a dead end. There was no freedom. If you met a white girl on a bus who'd gone to school with you and spoke to her, people would pass remarks. It was like Harlem. You had to be tough in Brixton. Some boys learned to box or wrestle to defend themselves; some cracked up under the strain. On the other side of the river it was not so bad, more cosmopolitan people I suppose. I trained at the Workshop under Robert O'Neill for four nights a week and managed to stay there two years by working in the day.

I had a terrible Cockney accent. Some people said it was twice as strong as other people's. But I started going around with some ex-public school boys and with the speech training it began to go. I was twenty and I thought I was going to be an actor in six months. But I was bad. I didn't even know how to stand properly. I was encouraged when one teacher said I had a lot of feeling expressed through the eyes. I stayed at the Workshop two years and got jobs through my agent, Pearl Connor. My first stage part was as Bret Charles in *Deep are the Pools* at the Grand Palais Theatre in Whitechapel in the East End. Bret is an American Negro who comes back from the war and falls in love with the white daughter of the house. The mother and father make life hell for him and the Sheriff takes him away and beats him. It was a good part.

Then I had four lines to say as an errand boy in a film, *Flame in the Street*. The fee was fourteen guineas but I wangled some overtime as an extra and came away after a few weeks with £189. I thought it was going to be easy for me, Sidney Poitier was at his peak and everybody said I was the English answer. I was getting part after part, although they were rarely more than four lines and always as a Negro or an immigrant.

Producers and directors often promised me parts which had nothing to do with my race but when it came down to actual casting for a play or film they never felt able to put into practice what they'd said previously. Then I ran into trouble. I wasn't getting any roles because every part was written for a West Indian accent, which was the trendy thing at the time, and I can't do a West Indian accent. I'm a black Englishman. My mannerisms and my character are different. The jobs stopped and I bummed around, living at home. I just didn't realize that script writers would be so daft as to write exclusively for West Indians.

Around this time I was deeply in love with a white girl and we wanted to marry but the girl didn't stand a chance. Her father told her that he preferred her to marry a criminal rather than a black; the mother did everything she could to stop it. Of course, the girl had to call it off. It was hard to live in a land where you were born and to find you couldn't love the person you wanted to. It really hurt.

I decided to take up folk singing – blues and gospel songs – and sang at parties and for friends. It didn't earn any money. I made a couple of demo discs and took them to record companies. One guy would say 'you're great', then his partner would turn you down. There would be big arguments about whether there would be public demand for a coloured heart-throb. This was the period when I met my wife, a white girl from the Isle of Man. Her parents and I get on well. Sometimes I meet in the street the mother of the girl I wanted to marry before and now she's as nice as can be because she's seen my face on television. I don't want to know. My wife encouraged me to get back into serious acting and I got a small part – twelve lines – in *Danger Man*. It brought in £100 for ten days work. The money's good when you're working but you should see the gaps!

I believed I was going to make it in a big way just because I was coloured. Poitier, Belafonte and Mathis went down well as heart-throbs because they were a symbol. Why not me? But the parts didn't come in and I had to go to work as a press operator, then a warehouseman. It was a bitter experience to be out of acting. Then I got a small part in a film called *Two Gentlemen Sharing*. It was a terrible film, treating the whites and blacks in London like cowboys and Indians. The whites would go slumming in the black area; there was rivalry between the races over women. It was never shown in this country but I heard it went down well in America!

But it was a break and then I got a part in *Softly, Softly* and a television producer said he would use me in roles which didn't have a racial context but – like the others – he didn't. I went to Tangier to do a travel commercial for African countries. I was a black playboy with an Aston Martin and beautiful birds. Then I had a bit in a sketch on television in *Barry Humphries' Scandals* in which I was a Negro who went to a clairvoyant and was told he would meet a tall white stranger. The 'stranger' turned out to be a polar bear.

I was cast as a Negro turning up at the Labour Exchange in Charlie Drake's *The Worker* series but this bit was cut out. Charlie said he'd try to use me as a non-coloured actor and he did. I was given the part of an MI5 scientist. There was a lay-off for four or five months until I got the part of Jimmy in Shelagh Delaney's play *A Taste of Honey*, produced by the Phoenix theatre company at Leicester. We played to packed audiences for three weeks and it was a very rewarding experience. There were love scenes between black and white and the audience enjoyed them. My next break was with the Prospect theatre company. I had the part of Frank Barber, Boswell's Negro servant, in *Boswell's Life of Johnson* and a couple of lines as the Watch in *Much Ado About Nothing*. This was a non-racial role: the whole cast play Mexicans anyway. The plays ran for ten weeks at the Edinburgh international festival. Actors say to me, 'When are you going to play Othello?' and I always reply 'After I've played Mark Anthony'. I wouldn't expect to play Richard III or a character from history like that because Richard wasn't a Negro. It's a very difficult problem – black actors must be given parts according to their ability but also you can't go against history.

And my characterizations and expressions are different from Africans and West Indians although I'm as black as they are. Just because my mother is brown-skinned it doesn't mean that she is any less English than a white person born in England. My friends often say to me that I'm 'not like the rest of them', but I have to point out that my skin is black so what's the real difference?

I have lived with colour prejudice all my life and when other blacks say I ought to read Malcolm X and think about Black Power I just shrug it off. I regard myself as a Welshman, because that's where I was born. I'm interested in me, in my career, and in my family. I am certain that one day I am going to make it into the big time. I'm happy and free as I am and I feel you cannot get anywhere by being prejudiced. Prejudice is only ignorance and fear. Up in Edinburgh, where there aren't many black people, I would be in a club and see a black man walk in. He would look around nervously but the minute he saw my face his eyes would light up and he'd relax. I suppose he felt that if I was accepted into the club it was also all right for him. This happened several times. We didn't need to speak. It was all a matter of visual acceptance.

I expect I will have to go on playing racial roles for some time. I don't mind as long as my work can draw people together, especially those people with a tendency to treat black people as evil. A pity, because I consider the best things I have done in my profession were non-racial. But unless I accept the racial roles there will be no real work as an actor because the public isn't yet ready to accept a black face where a white face is expected.

# 6. The holiday to end all holidays

Mervyn Bentham is forty-two and works for the General Post Office in London. A calm, thoughtful man and a practising Christian, he does not have the anger of the militants or the wildness of youth. Having been in Britain since 1957, worked and saved hard, he is what may be called a middle-class Negro. This is his story:

I was brought up in Oistin's Town, Barbados, and left school at sixteen without any certificates. I tried cabinet-making for a few months and then went to the USA as a contract war-worker in 1945. I was in North Carolina for four months in a wood-treating plant. We lived in premises attached to the factory and only went out for relaxation, mainly at week-ends. It was then I ran up against racism for the first time. In Wilmington several of us went into a store for some drinks, popped the bottles by the counter and started to drink. The store owner shouted 'You can buy it here but you can't drink it here', which astounded us as the whites were drinking in the place. We didn't move at first; then the owner went into the back and came back with a gun in a holster. We left! Another time in Georgia about a dozen of us out for a walk went into a hotel for a meal and we were immediately told we weren't allowed in there. We told them we were war production men but they sent us out. We told a policeman what had happened and he took us back in, pointed out to the hotel manager that we were entitled to food because we were war production men, and had documents to prove it, and they had better serve us. We got a good meal. I would like to have stayed on in the USA but, man, not in North Carolina! I would have gone to New York or somewhere. But the immigration authorities would not let us stay.

Back in the Barbados, I got a job as verger at Christchurch parish church on the strength of my having been a choir boy. It paid £5 a month and I had to prepare the church for services, register the baptisms, marriages and deaths and things like that. After four years in this job I became superintendent of the cemetery at £10 a month. It was a fairly responsible job and I had three people working under me. I stuck this for six years but my wages were extremely low. I thought there might be a chance of improving myself in Britain and then coming back to the West Indies with some qualifications. I wanted to train as a physiotherapist. So I came to London where friends had accommodation ready for me, and I got a job on the railways in Cricklewood, servicing carriages. This was 1958 and it paid about £8 a week. At nights and week-ends I studied a correspondence course on massage and electro-treatment and finished 75 per cent of the theory. Then I realized I had no capital to do the practical training in order to qualify or to set up on my own. I gave up. After three years with British Rail I went to the Post Office as a postman in the parcels section, which paid £9 15s. a week basic, but you can earn a lot more with overtime. Then I moved to the inland letters section as a sorter. I've met some racists working in the Post Office but I'd rather not talk about those incidents because I'm still working there. It would be a bombshell for me to tell you the story. It's not a healthy situation. But I've had some very nasty things happen to me outside.

For my first three years I lodged at the house of an English lady, Miss Howe, who treated us very nicely and the accommodation was good. Then I stayed in one-room apartments shared with a friend and then launched out on my own. I had one or two unpleasant experiences looking for accommodation. The moment you are seen coming to some houses, you knock, the door will open, and it will be slammed without a word being said. They've seen the face and that's that. On other occasions, people opened and when you asked what you wanted the reply was 'No accommodation'. This has happened on many an occasion going round and around. I don't think it's unfamiliar because it happens all the time. I wouldn't like to count the times

I've had this sort of rebuff. One evening in the Wood Green district I was refused about a dozen times.

Once I saw an advertisement in a shop window offering rooms to 'yellow people only'. I decided, well, I'll go. I knocked and the lady, who looked Indian, said, 'No, I don't want you. Didn't you see the advertisement?' I said, 'Can you describe who is a yellow person? Then I would understand why I shouldn't come.' I also said to her she was misleading the public and she should remove the advertisement. I offered to go and have it removed for her. She refused. I told the lady in the shop what had happened and suggested she should remove the notice and she said 'No. I'm paid for keeping it here and therefore I've got to keep it here.' Next day I went back and it was changed. It was changed from 'yellow people only' to 'No coloureds need apply'. (Such advertisements became illegal with the passing of the Race Relations Act in 1968.)

I have been on holiday in England once. Since then I always take my holidays in day outings to the seaside with my wife and little girl. We go off to Brighton or Southend on the train, coming back the same night. I went on holiday once, on a tour. With a friend and his wife, and me and my wife (we didn't have children then) we set out in a car for a tour of the South East – and since then I have never attempted to seek accommodation. We left here at noon, intending to get bed and breakfast wherever we were that night, and at nightfall we were in Bournemouth. We'd been around to about ten places and were all told 'Sorry'. The car became a little low in petrol so we went to a garage and the white manager there said 'I'll take you around; I'm sure I'll get you somewhere.' It was late September, hardly the peak of the holiday season. We only wanted boarding-house accommodation, not hotels. He took us to five places and came out with the answer every time: 'Sorry, they won't take you.' Whether he knew the managements or not I don't know. I think he did. When we asked him whether they were full up, he'd reply: 'Sorry, I can't get you in.' Eventually we decided to go into the back streets and my friend and I split up and eventually found a place that had accommodation. We stood there for fifteen minutes and eventually a chap came back and said 'All right, we'll have you'. We were well treated, the accommodation was good and we had a nice breakfast. When they are full up you usually see the sign 'Full' but I can't remember that we saw that once. I always understood accommodation was reasonably easy to get in late September. Next day we made sure we were near home at the end of the day and came back to our place. We never even stopped to ask for any accommodation. I decided that was the end. It might have been a bit defeatist but I decided that was the end. When my little girl is a bit older I might change my mind and try it; all the kids look forward to going on their holidays and I will have to fall in line. For myself I'm not worried. I've always planned that if things get better I don't see why my daughter can't spend her holidays in the West Indies. She wouldn't encounter all the nonsense we encounter here.

In my opinion she didn't well get into school before she was coming home with the old stories, they were calling her 'black this' and 'dirty black' and this kind of thing. She had been to a multi-racial pre-school play group before and that helped her enormously, the organizer was superb, one of the most understanding persons I have ever met in dealing with both races. When she started school she came home with stories about what she had been called. She didn't want to go to school after she was getting this treatment. I decided not to go to see the headmaster about it, because what could he do about it? That would only be putting extra pressure on him. I was prepared to talk to the child and try to get the child out of it. The child found a way out of it between the two of us. I told her, 'never mind what they say, you know what they are, they're white, you're black, your parents are black so you couldn't be born white. Their parents are white, so they couldn't be born black. There's no difference.' This is the thing I tried to impress on her. She was only five at the time and I was hoping it would stick into her little head. There are very few coloured kids at her school; I don't think it's because of the staff, they're extremely nice, especially the headmaster. But a lot of people don't want to send their children to Kentish Town Church of England school because it is not a modern school for a start and it's not very big. I really chose the school because it was on my way to work; the bus stop is just there and I could drop the child in and continue. The black kids are very much in a minority but I could not give you a reason for it, it probably is because it's not a modern type of building. In this area we've got Chinese, Pakistani, West Indian, the Irish, everybody.

What shook me more than anything else about coming to this country is in the church. I have been to St Thomas's – invited there as a matter of fact – to a men's fellowship. There was a time during the course of the evening when refreshments were served. I was sitting there alone (no one sat anywhere near me to say anything) but I felt quite happy. The sandwiches passed around and I was by-passed. I couldn't see how it was; I was the only coloured man there and the church was well lighted so they couldn't miss me! A chap came around with the tea, and included me, and then the sandwich man came back and said 'I'm sorry I by-passed you. I didn't mean to'. I said 'You can keep by-passing because I don't want your sandwiches.' That was in the church! I said, 'Why did you pass me? the chap with the tea didn't.' I came to my conclusion that he was one of those people. I don't see how he could have missed me; I was alone there sitting on the end. I think the chap with the tea must have hinted to him that I didn't get any sandwiches. I put him down as one of those people who intend to do those things.

I still go to church but I'm not very happy with the Anglican religion today. Some of my friends have complained often enough to me that at such and such a church they were told 'we don't appreciate you coming very often; my congregation don't like it.' It hasn't happened to me, but friends of mine in Birmingham, in Reading, they met with it. In Reading the chap told them straight, 'I would appreciate it if you didn't come back.' Another clergyman told a friend, 'I myself as a priest I have no objections to you coming but in the interests of everybody concerned I would advise you not to continue.'

Now I look back on my thirteen years in Britain I realize I should somehow have got those qualifications I intended to get when I first came here. I feel very strongly about the fact that I had to pack it up, because of the economic situation. I just couldn't work and get on with my study the way it should be done. I would have had to do a full-time practical course after the theory and I didn't see how I could do it without some financial backing. I'm very disappointed about that today.

I have met a bit of prejudice; it's worst at work. Occasionally you have to work with a chap who's more or less a Mosleyite or a Nazi; you'd be with him and get nothing but insults, dirty this or that; where you left your grass skirt? You got to put up with it actually, because it's no good complaining. They tell you 'you been assigned these duties and you got to work with them'. You've only got to step on a chap's corns to see exactly where he is or how far he'll go.

I have met very little prejudice at various evening institutes and workmen's colleges that I've attended. I could almost say none was shown to me. In my daily life as I go around you do get it. In a shop you go to be served and you are by-passed until you have to make some rude remark to be served. Sometimes you sit in a bus and you notice that unless that bus is actually filled you are sitting alone from the beginning to the end of your journey. Time and time again. But, as I say, I haven't met with a hell of a lot. In various organizations here you meet the odd chap you're introduced to and he says 'Hello' and that about the end of it. He never wants to say anything to you again.

To me racial prejudice is far more open today. You go anywhere and a chap tells you straight, 'I don't fancy coloured people.' This has only been in the last couple of years. Since you start to get it coming out both in politics, race relations and all these groups. At one time you'd go and a chap would talk to you and it's only somebody tell you afterward 'He doesn't like you chaps at all.'

Having gone through the lot now for thirteen years it would take something outstanding to say 'I'll run,' but I've got plans for going back. I don't fancy spending the rest of my life here. If I get my child through school here I wouldn't even like her to stay here because I feel the atmosphere is not pleasant enough. If she chooses to stay, then that's a matter for her. Coming here,

I'm not sorry, because of the experience I've got but it is far from what I understood it would be when I was leaving home. I worked with English people in Barbados, a lot of priests, and foolishly thinking you're going to meet the same type of person in your ordinary life here was a big mistake. You meet the kind of gentle man type there and here you meet the ordinary type who's willing to tell you what he thinks of you, and that's that. Will I ever really be able to go back? If, even now, I can do something which is valuable or that is needed I intend to go back.

# 7. The long, hard climb up

Glen English has a fairly unique view of racial attitudes in Britain. He came here from Jamaica in 1944, has worked his way up from nothing to a responsible, well-paid job, and in 1947 married a white girl he met in Leeds. They had three children, now grown up. In his twenty-six years in Britain Glen has met plenty of prejudice and discrimination because of his blackness, both at work and in his family life. Fortunately he has a placid but forceful nature, enabling him to choose whether to meet the racism head on or merely to shrug it off as bigotry and ignorance. His experiences leave him deeply convinced that prejudiced attitudes, even if they cannot be immediately broken down, can be worn away by patient argument and example, although he has come to the conclusion that about one in ten people in Britain seem incurably racist.

Glen was born in 1926 in Cuba, where his parents had gone from Jamaica to work temporarily on the sugar harvests. He was five when they returned home and he was able to start school against a congenial family background. He did well in his lessons and by the time he was fifteen was selected to help his teachers in return for their giving him private tuition. The schoolteachers wanted him to join their profession but he felt that he would rather work with his hands so he transferred to a technical school. Jamaica was a quiet place in those wartime days, most of the men being away in the British armed services or in America working in the munitions and food factories. Glen's father had died when Glen was nine and his mother made a small income by running a grocery store. The RAF recruiting office was just around the corner from Glen's technical school in Kingston. Most of the boys were signing on even if their studies were not complete and Glen could not resist the temptation either. He sailed to England in a well-guarded convoy in 1944. He said:

When I first came here there was a great deal of curiosity about people like me. Sometimes you could call it prejudice but I'm not sure. Most people hadn't seen a coloured face. One had to get used to it. If you were particularly sensitive you'd feel a bit of a charlie walking down the road and people turned to look at you. You tended to falter a bit. The servicemen I worked with were a marvellous bunch of companions but I'm afraid that as soon as they got back into civvy street their attitudes changed. I bumped into one chap in Leeds after the war with whom I'd had long discussions in the hangars and I greeted him just as I used to when we were in camp. But he had a girl on his arm and he suddenly coloured up to the roots of his hair and sort of exchanged greetings with me, but with one foot on the go, wanting to get off. I felt awfully self-conscious after, wondering if I'd done the right thing speaking to him, and then it began to dawn on me that there was this difference between when we were in camp together and when we were outside.

At a church in Devon while he was in the RAF Glen presented himself for communion. He had been a choir boy back in Kingston and was confirmed. As he filed past the vicar with the other communicants he was not offered the customary piece of bread, the clergyman merely touching his outstretched hand. No questions were asked, Glen did not make a fuss, but the event left him puzzled. 'In lots of cases I was made to feel different and to feel as though I didn't belong, and it would be better as if I wasn't there,' he said.

The examples of prejudice he met did not worry Glen unduly and when demobilization approached in 1947 he opted to stay in this country for he had heard from Jamaica that things were 'hard on the rocks'. He was a trained aero-engine fitter and began a pre-release draughtsmanship course. But once he had told the RAF of his intention to stay he was asked to pay for the cost of the course. The thought of being saddled with a big debt immediately he was demobilized unnerved him and he dropped out after ten months. He was told that if he was returning home to Jamaica the course was free, a decision which seemed to make little sense to him.

Glen resolved to become a draughtsman but it took him eighteen months to get a toehold. He had passed matriculation, taken most of the training course in draughtsmanship, and imagined he would get a job quite easily. Now married with one child, he did other jobs and went to night school during the period he searched in and around Leeds – this was during the post-war industrial boom – for the job he felt he was best suited to do. He comments:

I only got a draughtsman's job by a million-to-one fluke. Employers just wouldn't hear of taking me on. They would say: 'Where did you learn that sort of thing?' Usually you couldn't get past the commissionaires. It was most peculiar how I eventually got my job. It was a neighbour of the wife's mother who was a regular peacetime soldier in Jamaica and who knew of our marriage. The wife's mother was talking to him and he said his boss wanted a draughtsman. He mentioned it to the firm's managing director who said to come for an interview. Very, very reluctantly he said 'Well, we'll give you a chance.' It was pretty grim. He only gave me the chance because he thought that it pleased his boss, taking me on. Other people seemed to want to get their friends in instead of me and things were tense. There were attempts to discredit my work but I survived.

This was the big break Glen wanted and he never looked back. People previously had not thought he had the ability to do a skilled job such as a design draughtsman. They were willing to give him a job on a machine or sweeping up. He got along well with the men in the design shop drawing office, although he noticed they never invited him home. After four years there was a trade depression and he was asked to work in the machine shop to help out until things got back to normal. He was not keen to leave the drawing board but eventually agreed. He says:

Then I got a shock. I found that in the general sacking they finished about sixty or so in a very short time and they had sacked one of the fitters in the machine shop to make way for me. When I got there I found I had to do this man's job, and to do it more effectively perhaps. The men who had served under him were resentful of his going and hid just about every bit of tackle which could be used on the machines. There wasn't anything. I couldn't find a bit of machinery anywhere. It was hopeless. I knew roughly what to do but there was no help coming from anybody. I asked about things but no one seemed able to help. I didn't have any spanners because I'd been working in the office so I borrowed one. Someone reported me to the chap and he put his stuff away. It was grim. Anyway, we had a bit of a showdown about it and I went to see the machine shop foreman. He did a bit of shouting around the sections but the resentment was very acute. It went on for a few weeks. A European in my position might have got the same treatment it's true, but I also had to break down their prejudices. Towards the end of the six months I was in the shop things improved. Then I was transferred to progress chasing but I could see this might go on for a long time and wasn't doing my career much good so I went and got myself another job as a draughtsman. After a year the old firm asked me to come back which I did, and I stayed ten years, finishing up as planning engineer.

Glen moved to a factory in Bradford, feeling he had got as far as was possible with the smaller firm, and he wanted more security. He remained there four years until he took up a new post as a draughtsman instructor at a government training centre.

A piece of discrimination which does credit neither to the insurance company nor the trade union happened to Glen in 1960. Through his union, the Allied Society of Draughtsmen and Engineers, now merged into DATA, a company offered cheap car insurance to members of the union at 15 per cent discount. Glen applied and he was quoted £8 below what he was paying at the time but on the form which he had to complete was an item 'Place of birth' which Glen answered honestly. The company wrote to say that they would not accept his policy because he was not born in this country so Glen, who at the time was a minor union official responsible for collecting the dues, asked a senior union official to take the matter up.

Letters went backwards and forwards for weeks until finally a letter came from the district organizer saying: 'We've done all we can in this case and it does seem that if you insist they will cancel all the policies for the 3,000 members.' They said it was entirely up to me, but he put it to me, was it fair to jeopardize other people's poliices? In other words he was throwing the onus back on me. I decided not to pursue it but I resigned from all union work.

In 1969 the Race Relations Board stamped out the practice of 'loading' the car insurance policies of people on the grounds of overseas birth – at least by companies which are members of Lloyds motor underwriters association.

It is the little things that a sensitive black person notices about a white person's actions that are often hurtful:

For instance, even when I was doing quite well, a man would come into the office for information and I'm the only adult in the office and he would ask the lad who was working for me on the next board the question he wanted. I would stand and watch this happen. Then the lad would say, 'You'd better speak to Mr English; he's in charge.' Then the man would say he was sorry and come to me. But his first impulse is either that he isn't going to ask me or I won't have the answer to what he wants. This used to have all sorts of funny effects. People used to walk into my office and think you are out of place in there or you're some hell of a guy to be in there in the first place. Their reactions after they'd been in for a while used to tell you this. But there would be others who would come in and take it, as it were. You would have to be superhuman not to be conscious of this. I'm not normally a chap who gets on his high horse about anything; like a draughtsman I usually weigh the pros and cons and think, well, is there a reason for this? But when this happens, most times I have usually to come to the conclusion that under other circumstances it might not have happened. It is only then that I feel that I ought to take some sort of action.

Has this quarter-century of inner struggle against prejudice made Glen English a different man from the one he might have been? Perhaps more mature, broadminded and a cleverer draughtsman? This is what he feels:

I think I would have been a worse draughtsman than I am because of this. I might have tended to slacken. I find that because I've had to put myself out to convince people – and I've had to do it the subtle way – I've had to do things that little bit better. I think it has made me a better person. I've had to push harder. I've never wanted to be found wanting. My general attitude to people has been the area in which I think I've made most improvement as a result of this attitude towards me. I studied a lot and tried to acquire some culture so that nobody could have the laugh on me as being the bloke who didn't know. But I found you're still coloured and anybody can come and militate against you on that ground alone, irrespective of what you know or what you are. If you go into the factory shop and meet a chap who's giving you a slight on the grounds of colour by what he's said or done, and you know he's not looked after his life and perhaps he's half the man you are, and it hurts you more that he should have this attitude to you on the one basis alone that neither you nor he can do anything about. But on the things that matter he doesn't even begin to count and yet he is playing this game. One thing I have learned in this country is to use words to hit back rather than weapons. And do you know, I could count on the fingers of one hand the number of times I've been invited to the home of any workmate. To me this is the ultimate: if a man will say 'Come to our house and have tea,' then as far as I'm concerned he's accepted you as a social equal. It might not turn out well but he's done it. They'll go to the pub with me any time but not to their home . . . it's this little leap across which they find difficult.

At a dance in Leeds Glen met a miner's daughter, a tall, blonde girl dalled Rita. She had been to school with a coloured girl and was completely without prejudice. Her mother didn't oppose the marriage but her father opposed her marrying anybody. She asked him if she could bring Glen home to tea as they were hoping to be married, not telling him her boyfriend was black, and he refused. He signed the consent form and didn't go to the wedding. When a relative told him after the reception that his son-in-law was black he fainted. When he recovered he said he never wanted to see her again. The young couple struggled against financial difficulties like any newly-weds but Glen had the additional tough task of getting work in a racially prejudiced society.

Rita was early baptized with racial abuse. She was standing on a bus with Glen when a woman who was seated said to her husband 'Get up and let that woman sit down; she's expecting.' Whereupon the man said, 'What! When she's with a blackie! No fear!' Glen told her as they got off the bus that they would get a lot of incidents like that. One of them caught Rita on the wrong foot: she was standing in a bus queue and saw a Negro whom she thought was a friend of her husband. She looked at him hard so that she could greet him if she was right. Then a white woman standing next to the Negro turned angrily on Rita and shouted: 'Don't stare at him! he's every bit as good as your husband!'

When her embarrassment had passed the incident cheered Rita up greatly. She had too many other worries over the flat, food and babies to get overwrought about prejudice but the ugly moments added to the problems of young married life. When Glen was unemployed she worked at a little factory at the end of the road and had to put up with a stream of taunts about being married to a black man.

It soon got round the works that Rita was 'the girl down the road with the coloured baby'. The fitters gave Rita the hardest time she had ever encountered, making rude remarks as she went from one office to another. 'Couldn't you find a white man then?' the workers would snigger. One morning there was a picture in the *Daily Mirror* of an African in full war dress and they pinned it over her desk with the inscription 'Is this your mother-in-law?' Rita's reaction was to go into the works and declare: 'If you men have nothing better to do than bully me, call me names, then you really ought to be ashamed of yourselves.' This frontal attack on the men's childish behaviour had the effect of quietening them.

Probably more wearing was the constant breaking down of friendly relationships with other women once they discovered her husband's race, and the hard climb back to a new friendship. This showed up in hospital when she gave birth to her children. Glen would come in to visit her and when he left a situation would develop.

You'd turn to the girl in the next bed and you'd find she's very cool with you [says Rita]. The women would get into a little huddle and then one of them would broach the subject: 'Is he your husband then?' I hope so, I'd say. 'Are you married to him?' Then you've to start to build up a friendship again, a friendship that they took for granted before was all gone. Then the women would come up with all the usual tales about girls who marry coloured men are oversexed but by the time you're ready to leave hospital you've made one or two friends. You realize then that they are the friends you would have made anyway. And then if anyone new comes into the ward you have to face it again.

Mr and Mrs English feel that one reason black people

congregate in areas like Chapeltown and Burley in Leeds is that they are not able to cope with the constant 'brainwashing' sessions which are needed to maintain communication with white people. They have become used to it but in the early years when they were trying to find an identity it was a continual strain.

Their children were among the first to enter the local schools, meeting the inevitable boyish taunts. It is the consequences of these taunts which can sometimes be more hurtful than the actual incident. The eldest boy, Glenroy, came home one day and said: 'They've been calling me blackie at school. Am I black? Am I black? I'm not black! Look! Dad's black but I'm not black!' His mother told him that if he was not called that it would be something else. It needs a phlegmatic temperament for a father to hear that and not be stung into action. The problems really started in their teens. 'They certainly went through hell,' says Glen. 'When the eldest lad got to about fifteen he wanted to do the same things as his friends, like taking girls to the films, and the girl's parents wouldn't let him.'

His great romance was with a girl whose parents kept the local chip shop. He was just leaving grammar school and the girl was very keen on him. The parents seemed very reasonable and allowed their daughter to court the boy for a while but then the parents said they were coming under pressure from their customers about the affair. 'They're a nice family (meaning the Englishes) but what about when she has any children?' the customers would say as they salted their chips. Suddenly the shop-owner decided he had had enough and stopped it. The girl thought about it for a fortnight and then told the Englishes' son that they had better break off as it was causing too much trouble. The boy told his parents: 'That's it! I'm never going to ask another English girl out.' He later married a black girl who had emigrated at the age of eight. The younger boy married a white girl.

Glenroy left grammar school with one 'A'-level and four 'O'-levels and wanted to work in a bank. At the first bank he tried he went along with two other boys and they helped each other fill out the application forms. The two white boys got jobs: Glenroy was rejected. He followed this up with applications to all the banks in Leeds and was turned down by every one. His father, who was then serving on the Leeds International Council, a forerunner of the Community Relations Committee, had inquiries made which showed that the banks would not employ coloured clerks as a matter of policy. That a young man born and bred in Leeds, the son of a Leeds-born woman and a Jamaican-born man, who had passed with credit through a grammar school only to be rejected for a lowly post in a bank, was just one of the reasons why the Race Relations Act had to be passed in 1968 to make such discrimination illegal.

# 8. It's the women who suffer

One of the most interesting and important characters in the black community is the West Indian mother. Because of the way her society has developed, from the slave days when she was regarded by the entrepreneurs as merely a breeder of more slaves, right up to the present economic depression in the Caribbean, an unfair burden always falls on her. After they are born, she is both mother and the father of her children, as this story illustrates. This woman spoke with great frankness and asked us not to print her name. She told us:

Forty-one years ago I was born in St Vincent, West Indies, where I lived till 1960 when I came to England. I am the eldest of five children, three boys and two girls. When I started school we lived at home with my mother and father. My younger brother was three and I was five at the time. My mother used to be at home all the time and dad was working as a joiner when he could get work. If he wasn't doing joinery he used to work the piece of land we had about two miles from the house. Auntie Sybil lived next door and Cousin Doreen lived just across the way. We used to go over and stay with Auntie Sybil when both my parents went to town or to the market. Sybil used to help me with my reading because my mother never had time and anyway Sybil was much better at books.

In 1940 when I was eleven and my brother eight my father left home and went to sea. My mother and Aunt Sybil told us he had gone to work on a battleship because Britain was fighting a war. Aunt Sybil, Doreen and the rest of the neighbours used to come round very often then because my Ma was always worried and they sat talking about the war, while we children would play about in the moonlight in the yard or play hide-and-seek under the house. Although Doreen and Sybil and Doreen's brother used to help my mother with the land as my father was away, my mother made me do a lot of work too. My brother was reaching the age when he could sit for scholarship and go to school in town so Ma had to make sure she was able to support him at school if he passed the scholarship. So apart from keeping three goats, I two and he one, my brother and I also planted lettuce, tomatoes, and such things near the house. My mother did not have to spend much for food because she could get provisions from the garden or from a cousin's land and get fish from Mr Thomas and his son down at the beach. But she had to spend for shoes and clothes for us and things for the house. We very rarely ate meat. We used to kill a fowl once in a while on a Sunday – but we stopped because Ma had to sell as many eggs as she could.

My mother began worrying more and more about whether Desmond would pass his scholarship or not, and about my father who we were hearing from less and less. I think she began to feel she couldn't cope as well as before so I had to be spending more and more time away from school either to look after my mother or to go to the garden and fetch provisions for the market. Anyway, I was a big girl at twelve and because I was in Standard 7 without a hope of going to High School in town, my mother took me away from school to stay at home and work. Desmond sat the scholarship exam and passed, which meant that his school fees were paid, but Ma had to provide the books, his school uniform and bus fares every month or boarding fees for a boarding house in town. If Desmond hadn't passed and mum had to pay the $20 fees every term Desmond would never have had secondary education. Ma decided that since I was at home helping her work the land and since it was cheaper to have Desmond board in town, she would let Desmond stay in town and I would go for the two younger ones, my younger brother and sister who were living with grandma on the other side of town. The boy was six-and-a-half and the girl four, big enough to help themselves and be of assistance to Ma and me.

The very week I was to go for them a letter came saying daddy was dead. He was one of many lost in a boat. Word went round the island that two people from Trinidad and one from St Lucia were lost as well. The whole village was upset and as for Ma she couldn't bear it. All that time she was worrying, as if she knew something was going to happen. Ma went to town and told Desmond who like the rest of us had not seen his father for four years. It put Desmond off for a while, but possibly because it was all happening so far away he soon forgot about what it must mean to him. I went to grandma to collect Stephen and Grace and I told grandma the bad news. I stayed with grandma for about a week and then I came away with Stephen alone. It would have broken the old lady's heart to take them both away. Soon after that Ma said to me that I was becoming a big woman and I no longer had a father; she still had the young ones, including Desmond at secondary school to look after, so I should go and learn a trade – dressmaking – as well as helping her in the land.

So at fifteen I started to learn dressmaking with a lady about two miles from my home. When I started there were four other apprentices taking lessons. The lady in charge was very good. She worked us hard, but she knew of my father's death and so she used to allow me enough time to go with my mother to get provisions and go with them to the market. Ma was getting more and more satisfied with my progress and now I was a big girl she could do all the things she felt she alone had to do because dad wasn't there. So, soon enough, with Desmond home for vacation periods and his friends helping on the land, and Ma and I doing what we could, we coped very well.

Two of the girls who did dressmaking with me also taught at the Sunday school. The owner of the shop and our dressmaker instructor was a member of the Mothers' Union of the local R.C. Church. I used to go with them sometimes to their Sunday school class. Every so often their boy-friends would come and meet them to go out. Julia's boy-friend was the head altar-boy at the church. I can remember leaving them that particular Sunday and wondering what Ma would think if she knew I was going out with friends who had boy friends. After all, Ma and I had never spoken about sex or boys or marriage. The only thing she kept on saying was, you are a big woman, now remember always to be the sort of girl I brought you up to be. Don't go and bring shame on me and your father, especially with your brother studying in town. The following week at work the conversation was about boy meets girl practically all week. Then the Sunday I went with them to Sunday school and Julia's boy brought his friend who took a great interest in me. When Sunday school broke up I tried to shake him off in case someone saw me and went to tell Ma.

I was meeting that boy for quite a few Sundays when a woman who knows Aunt Sybil saw us holding hands and walking down the road and went and told Aunt Sybil who got very worried and ran over and told Ma. That night Ma never stopped quarrelling. She said just about everything including: If I was going to go to Sunday school with those jezebels to look for a man I was sure not leaving the house on Sundays any more. So my boyfriend used to meet me after work at the dressmakers and I used to go out with him. When I got home late I used to tell my Ma that Mrs Dee (the dressmaker) had a big order that we had to finish off urgently and so we were asked to stay on. I was seeing my boyfriend like that for months and my Ma never found out. In the end I had to tell her because I became pregnant. Now that was really terrible. It would have been so much better if I could have been seen with Albert before it all happened. It would not have been so shocking for everyone and I am sure if Ma had accepted him it would not have happened that way. Now she was slamming me and saying after all she had to go through to see me become a big girl look at how I repaid her. It also made her think about dad again, saying if your Father was here this would have never happened. I felt very awful at having hurt my mother so much because I don't think she understood I still loved her very much in spite of the fact that I was grown up and become a woman myself. But at the same time I cursed her for denying me the right to have the man I loved and whose child I was bearing. For months Ma wouldn't let Albert come near the house. And then when the child was born Ma let me take Albert home to see her and the child.

Albert was working at a store in town at the time and so we

both thought it might help if he gave up that job and came to help me and my mother work the land. My mother agreed and before very long Albert came to live with us. This arrangement worked for a while, but then we found we couldn't get enough from the land to provide clothes and food for all of us and to help Desmond who was still at school. In fact things got so bad that we had to sell more and more eggs and buy cod-fish (New foundland salt fish) for the family. We rarely ate meat. Butter was expensive, and the little we got for the bananas and cocoa and yams could not provide clothes for us and books for the children. Albert found another job in town and worked at that for about two years. Meanwhile I took up dressmaking again, sewing at home this time. Albert tried to save some money so that he and I could get married and build a little house. He wasn't doing too badly when his mother died and he had to spend the little he had saved. About six months after he buried his mother he went to Trinidad to work in the oil fields. I was one month pregnant with my second girl when he left. Albert kept on writing and sending money to me. Desmond finished school and got a job in town. He came back and lived at home for three months and then went to live in town altogether.

Cousin Doreen and several other people from our area left for England in 1958. She found a job in London and when she had settled down wrote persuading me to leave the children with Ma and Aunt Sybil and come to England. I thought about it for long time and then decided that Anne, the younger girl was old enough to leave behind so I started making plans to come. I saved some of the passage money myself and Ma borrowed the rest from the people for whom Desmond worked, signing over the land as security.

I came to England in 1962 and since then I am still trying to decide what has hit me. We arrived by boat at Southampton and came on by train to London. I expected Doreen to meet me but she was nowhere to be seen. I stood around like the rest of new arrivals feeling strange, cold and lost. Then a chap from Trinidad came up to me and said he had a van and would I like to be taken to my address. I gave him Doreen's address in Clapton and then he hurriedly explained that it was not exactly round the corner, so would I come to Acton with the people he had just picked up. I said I would, so about an hour later we finally turned up at that address in Acton. The owner of the house was white and I was to learn later that she constantly provided accommodation for people in my position till other accommodation was found. I stayed at that house for five weeks while I learned how London worked, how people behaved in London and how for people like me life was one long day's work with some breaks longer and more varied than others. In the course of those five weeks I met some people from back home who helped me to find Doreen. When I eventually caught up with her I discovered that she could not find me accommodation in the house she and others were renting.

Meanwhile the white neighbours of my white host had complained to the police and the public health authorities about the 'endless' number of black people coming and going in that house and she was given a week to get some of us out of there. This really shook me and I was even more surprised by the unfriendliness and nasty looks that I got from those people around. I have never felt so alone in all my life. But with meeting people I knew back home I was able to stay with one person one week and another person another week till I found a room to rent and bought the things I required. One of the girls in that multi-occupied place I stayed at found me a job at her factory doing packing. I opened my first pay-packet and found £9 3s. 0d. My first reaction was to convert it into dollars or rather West Indian currency, so I thought of it as roughly $40. But I soon had to stop doing this because when I went home and paid £3 rent, bought food for the next week and bought an old coat at a secondhand shop I did not have any money for bus fares the next week let alone anything to send to Ma for her and the children. Even when I began doing piece-work which paid more I still found myself in arrears with the rent every time I sent money home for Ma to pay off the passage loan.

Winter came and I had to buy oil heaters and warm clothes so for weeks Desmond's boss back home was taking money out of

Desmond's wages as regular repayments of the loan. This go
Desmond furious and it got me and my Ma real worried.
thought at any moment now I'll hear Desmond has lost the jo
and the people are going to sell the piece of land to get bac
their money. I went to see Doreen and for a while she helped m
out with food so that I could pay the rent and send the rest o
the money to my mother. Several times I felt I could just give up
Several times I would have got on a plane and gone right back i
only I had the money. I longed for my children, I was worrie
about my mother's health. I was sick and tired of doing thi
boring job for so many hours and coming home to a cold
crummy room which I could not even make brighter. I used to g
downstairs and watch TV in one of the girls' rooms but I usuall
ended up falling asleep.

I inquired around for months about whether or not I could b
employed as a dress machinist but no one would have me. I
the end I decided rather than go and watch television with th
girls I would sit and do some embroidery making place mats
chair covers and such things. I scraped to find money for materia
and started on it. After a few weeks I brought some finishe
articles to work and sold them to people at work. Soon thei
friends saw and liked what I produced and I was asked to mak
more and more. As a result things began to look up for me but i
also caused lots of confusion at work, with the white women. The
used to like to take pity on me before. They saw me as someone
they could help, someone who had to thank them for favours
Now with my sewing they started saying: 'She sells much mor
in here than what she sells outside; and yet she wants to gra
every bit of overtime. There is a greedy black bitch.'

This caused any amount of rows at work, black against white
I was damned well not going to tell that crowd my business
because I had already gotten wise to them. When I first came
still thought whites were somehow superior because every whit
man back home was treated as superior. He didn't even have t
make out like he was. But the few weeks after I landed in thi
place taught me a lot. My poor mother and I consoled ourselve
about dad's death. After all he was fighting for the 'mothe

country'. White people of every sort back home expect and enjoy all sorts of privileges, and now you come to the 'mother country' they want to treat you like you're dirt. Anyhow I continued to do my overtime and to sell my embroidery. Pretty soon mother was able to pay off the loan and to have a bit more money to spend on the children.

The house in which I lived was so run down I decided as soon as I could I'd go and find a better room somewhere. The white landlord turned up to collect his rent every Friday evening but nothing was done to the house by way of repairs. Looking back on it now I am sure fifteen shillings a week rent for that little room would have been plenty. In fact we were all so glad to have a place to come home and sleep in that we did not dare try and have the rent reduced. After a year in that little room I found myself another room. That second house was cleaner, it had a decent bathroom and it had two kitchens for everybody and not the one kitchen on the ground floor as in the other house. The room above that new room was occupied by a chap from Jamaica. He had been in England since '55 and certainly knew the ropes. We got on well together and he soon found me a job where he worked, this time doing assembling. Here I got eleven pounds a week. I started saving to have my eldest daughter join me here. Jackie was turning thirteen and finishing at school back home. She and Ma had stopped hearing from Albert. I wrote to Desmond and he agreed to lend some money towards Jackie's passage. I borrowed some from my friend upstairs and put with what I had saved.

Jackie came over and Ma kept the smaller girl with her. When Jackie arrived I think she found both me and the world around her quite strange. She was very surprised to learn that I had arranged for her to be admitted to secondary modern school here to do two years before starting work. I soon discovered that quite a lot of what I was taking for granted was causing Jackie great problems. The first few weeks we spent talking about home and my trip and her trip and the sort of work I had done and people I had met since I arrived. But once we had gone over that time and again Jackie began to feel extremely homesick, not even eating. I got her off to school and this created even more problems. Though she was as grown up if not more than the others in her class she felt out of place for a number of months. I came home one evening and found her on the bed crying, her eyes bulging. After hours of persuading she told me that she couldn't understand her teacher and he couldn't understand her; the other children were laughing at her; she couldn't stand the school dinners; she was bored with coming and sitting at home waiting till I came home. She cried and cried and then said she was not going back to school. I spoke to her and she was relieved by my promise to let her stay with some children down the street after school till I called for her. I had to do this though I would have preferred to have her come home and make a meal for both of us.

I left home at seven to go to work and got home at 6.30. It never occurred to me that Jackie could have done everything but go to school during those hours until one day a letter arrived saying would I come to the school. I went one afternoon and the headmistress asked why I was keeping Jackie at home; adding that her absence had been noticed off and on over the last three weeks. This came as a shock to me and the Head was even more shocked when I told her that as far as I knew Jackie came to school every day Monday to Friday. I found out soon afterwards that Jackie and the girls with whom she was permitted to stay after school used to play truant, go to the parks, to the swimming baths and on bus rides. As a result I gave Jackie quite a telling off and prevented her from going to join those girls after school or being seen with them at all. Her answer to this was to make remarks about my man upstairs and what had happened to her father? I think she began to see me as a different person and I certainly saw her as someone to be controlled. Jackie and I had quite a bit of a 'set-to' from time to time, in fact too much for my liking; so I decided to tell my 'man' upstairs what was going on. We discussed the situation quite a bit and then decided he and I would marry each other. Jackie became very bad-tempered the moment I mentioned anything about this marriage. She kept on saying she could not support me in this until I tried to find her father in Trinidad, no matter how good to me my husband-to-be was. Though I could see her point of view I was not prepared to go to Trinidad and since I was away from Albert for so long, did not know his address and he could not be bothered to write home, I could not tell whether he was still in Trinidad or not. Jackie's relationship with me soon became one of woman to woman and she really made me weep when I remembered how I behaved towards my own mother at Jackie's age.

However, James and I got married and we moved into a two-bedroom flat, taking Jackie with us. Jackie was not catching up at school as well as I would have liked and yet she suddenly had a craze for youth clubs and discoteques. Now I know what these places are like and no matter who says what I don't think they are the places for young girls, especially people like Jackie who need to be helped with their school work rather than provided with boy-friends. People like Jackie come here as innocent children but the bright sparks round here, you cannot control them, and it seems to me that whatever the youth club teaches them it does not teach them respect for parents. To begin with James used to tell me 'stop being so hard on the girl she needs to grow up round here with her friends, and the youth club is one of the places they meet one another'. I was never satisfied with that because I know it could bring trouble. Jackie finished school and started evening classes in typing and shorthand. But she never did go every time she left here to go to evening classes.

Any time she thought I would not let her go somewhere in the evening she never asked – she simply said she was going to a class of some sort. Before long boys started calling for her at the flat. My husband observed this for a while and pretended it was all very well. But soon Jackie began going out more and more and my husband started on me. Anytime he wanted to pick a row or any time I showed my dissatisfaction to him about anything he would say: 'I am already supporting your mother and your child at home, and this fully grown woman you've got here. The day she brings another mouth for me to feed I am getting right out of it.' Naturally, I had to agree with him and every time I spoke to

Jackie she refused to talk to me. Now she has stopped talking to my husband completely.

Bringing up children in this country is anything but fun. I can remember one day Jackie cheeked my husband and he stormed out. I went to her and slapped her face. She had a tussle with me and then reminded me that she could call the police and have me charged for fighting her. This sort of thing must break parents' hearts when you think that a society gives children that sort of power over you; children whom you have made great sacrifices to bring up well and who no longer want to go the right way. Jackie has left home now and is on her own as far as I am concerned. She shares a flat with a girl-friend who does typing too. I know she is courting like mad but I only hope she is independent enough to fix her business right. She still writes to Ma, but she hasn't told Ma she has left home. I have been tempted many times to write and tell Ma all that has gone on but I just couldn't. Despite everything, Ma sees me as someone who has failed. If I told her she is bound to say that I have also failed my daughter who was her trusted friend and first grand-daughter and who she is convinced would have fared well left with her gran.

All of that and all the other minor daily insults and injuries, the constant sweat and toil and nothing to show for it makes me hate this place more and more daily. Why don't I go back? Go back to what? People are not emigrating to Britain any more. In fact more are going back every year. To go back one must go back with plenty because my Ma is finding it a darned sight more difficult to make do now with the little she had to make do with eight years ago.

# 9. How many punishments are enough?

The Tylers are a Jamaican family who live in an East London borough. Mr Tyler has, by a woman other than his wife, two children whom he maintains in Jamaica. Mrs Tyler also has two children, by a man other than Tyler, whom she maintains in Jamaica. The couple had a son, Martin, living in Jamaica with Bob Tyler's mother. Bob Tyler was made aware of his mother's failing health, and being dissatisfied with Martin's progress in school anyway, thought it best to have the boy join him in London. Martin came and joined Jenny, his London-born sister: Jenny is now four and Martin twelve.

Mrs Tyler, five months pregnant and out of work, was receiving £5 15s 0d. from Bob for housekeeping when she discovered £2 missing from her purse one day. 'Oh! my God, it's not Martin pinching again? I hope the boy hasn't gone and spent all my money.' She anxiously awaited Martin's return from school and directly he was inside the door said to him: 'Martin, you took my money out of my purse.' Martin admitted it and dashed out of the house. His mother immediately imagined the worst and Martin had in fact blown the £2 with his friends. When Martin had still not shown up by 7 p.m. Bob and Mary Tyler decided to go looking for him; they combed the streets for four hours before the police caught up with them. Martin had been found at a shopfront shaking with fright and crying. He told the policeman who saw him that he had run away from home because he had to get a beating, without saying why he deserved the flogging.

He was taken to the police station where he gave information about himself. The police then contacted Bob Tyler and asked him to go to the station to collect his son. At the station, Mr Tyler was warned not to beat the boy but take him home, give him a meal and send him to bed. Back at the house the father took Martin to his mother who produced a rubber strap, flogged Martin – rebuking him very sternly at the same time – and sent him to bed.

Martin was doing P.E. at school next day when the teacher saw traces of blood on his shirt. Looking closer the teacher found weal marks and cuts on his back, shoulders and chest. The boy explained how he had been beaten by his mother the night before. The school doctor was brought in and Martin was sent to hospital where he was treated and discharged. The school informed the police and Bob and Mary Tyler were soon arrested and charged with cruelty to a child occasioning him grievous bodily harm.

A woman police constable investigating the case recommended to the court a 'fit person's order' for both Martin and Jenny. Bob and Mary Tyler and the children appeared in court, the 'fit person's order' plea was upheld which meant that both children were taken into the care of the children's department. The parents were perplexed at this and thought it a great injustice. Moreover they were convinced that such action having been taken, the matter was closed. They were shattered therefore when they received summonses to appear before the magistrate to answer the charge of occasioning grievous bodily harm.

A probation officer conducted a report on the background of that case which took into account: (1) the fact that Mrs Tyler was a staunch 'Church of God' devotee who believed that if the child engaged in pilfering he had the devil within him and by beating the boy one expels the demon; (2) that having to support this family on £5 15s. 0d. per week as well as Martin's brother and sister in the West Indies, she wished to impress upon the boy the seriousness of his deed; (3) that having spent four hours searching for the boy, distraught and anxious as she was – and five months pregnant – she was tired, upset, and angered, lost her temper and beat the boy much more severely than she normally would; (4) the fact that they were hard-working people who had never come in contact with the police before and found the whole situation very distressing; (5) that ordinarily both children are very well cared for despite the very great sacrifices each parent had to make.

The court, however, showed itself unable to look beyond the piece of rubber and the doctor's report. Little interest was shown in the upright characters of the parents or indeed in the factors that make having £2 stolen by her twelve-year-old boy such a crime as far as that mother was concerned. The only words of consolation Bob and Mary Tyler heard were: 'In this country we protect children from parents like yourselves. I sentence you both to six months' imprisonment.'

Mrs Tyler went into a state of shock on hearing the sentence and verged on a mental break-down. Bob Tyler could not comprehend the reasoning behind any law that imprisons parents because they beat their child under those circumstances. He explained over and over again that in Jamaica the boy would himself feel and would be told he was justly beaten, a beating which should serve as a deterrent to him in future situations.

For Bob Tyler the six-months sentence, great as it was, could be borne much more easily than his knowledge that 'his authority had been taken to court and denied him'. Confused as they were, Bob and Mary Tyler cooperated fully with the probation officer, much as they questioned the right of the probation service and the children's department to 'meddle' in such a domestic concern.

The structure of family life in the West Indies is one which allows for great variations of blood relationship extending far beyond the single family unit of parents and siblings. Uncles, aunts, nephews, nieces, sons of nephews and nieces, cousins of cousins, all form part of the extended family unit. The extended family could be called upon at any time to play a supportive role, operating as it does at this intermediate level of family life. Children accept and respect members of this large family; they look forward to receiving gifts from them and see it as normal to be requested by them to run errands or help with work. Children live with them quite happily if arrangements within the single unit family necessitate it. The children are assured a home and are treated on an equal basis as siblings.

As we demonstrate elsewhere in this book many fathers have

had to leave home to find work either in other islands or abroad. During the father's absence mother and children could count on necessary assistance from the extended family, i.e. from relations no matter how distant. In a community with such ready-made support, based on family groupings, it is the norm rather than the exception to have children separated from parents for any length of time and with no recognizable ill-effects. Children brought to England out of such a situation, however, have continued to pose problems to parents, teachers, and children's departments.

Martin Tyler was left with his grandmother at the age of three. He seemed to cope very well, being one of several grandchildren in that household. Having developed a strong emotional relationship with his grandmother he did not welcome the prospect of leaving her to join people in England of whom he had little more than photographic images or memory. On arriving in Britain Martin behaved in what his parents thought was an extraordinary way. Mr Tyler obviously expected him to have remembered the father of his infant days and to relate to Mary Tyler as his own mother.

Martin was, however, restrained and shy, not communicating very much at home. He was confident among his friends at school and down the street, only to 'clam up' again when he returned home. He was wary of his newly-acquired parents' claim to want to love and protect him. In Mrs Tyler's words: 'He told lies and started stealing things, such things he did not need. Even now the boy is too much of a little schemer.'

Mary Tyler seemed constantly unaware of the tensions young Martin was under. She attributed his petty pilfering, his dishonesty to the fact that Bob Tyler's mother 'let him have too much of his own way back home'. With the best of intentions she set out to correct the boy's wrongdoings by imposing the discipline she believed he lacked. Martin, for his part, was unwilling to accept this from someone who was not his mother – as far as he was concerned he had been brought up to think of his grandmother as his mother – and with whom he had no bond of emotion or friendship. Mary Tyler's corrective efforts simply served to harden and compound Martin's behavioural problems.

West Indian parents in general expect children to act responsibly at a very young age. Martin ought to have known what it means to have only £5 15s. coming in and have £2 of it stolen to spend – as a West Indian puts it – on 'stupidness'. Mary Tyler prides herself in giving him all he needs – materially speaking she does. Like so many other parents she feels it's all thrown back at her when she is confronted with the sort of behavioural problems which suggest – even if she does not understand it – that the emotional stability is lacking. Here is a woman trying to bring up her son in the best manner known to her but genuinely ignorant of the needs of her boy. Acting in what she believed to be his best interests she got carried away and caused him bodily injury. Did six months' imprisonment enable her to understand his problems and needs more readily? Could the children's department itself meet those needs by placing Martin into what potentially is a situation of greater emotional conflict? Did that court consider the nature of the future relationship between Bob and Mary Tyler and their two children when (hopefully) they are reunited?

Martin's crime was considered enormous within the family because Mary Tyler needed the £2 to send for the upkeep of children in Jamaica. Further implications of a prison sentence were that for six months back in the Caribbean two grandmothers each caring for two children were denied financial support from the Tylers. Those four children would not have been taken into care there, even if they became the collective responsibility of the community around them during those six months.

# 10. A view from the black underworld

*Little has been discovered about the black underworld in British cities, but in this interview between Gus John and a young crook we have called 'Mike' there is a rare glimpse of some of the causes of black criminality. Mike's argument that crime among immigrants is, on average, no higher than the indigenous population, is well corroborated by crime statistics. The interview is transcribed from a tape-recording.*

GUS JOHN: Mike, you came to this country from the West Indies seventeen years ago and you have seen Handsworth develop. You went through school here, you started work here, you've seen white people of the area, you've seen black people in the area; you've seen the conflicts that have arisen during the early years of immigration. What's it been like?

MIKE: When I first started infant school, you know, this was in 1955. I was the only little coloured boy there in the school, you know. At times this could be quite an advantage and at times it could be quite a disadvantage, let's say sixty/forty per cent of the time a disadvantage, because you were always an object of ridicule or, you know, some form of comical jest more or less to the other pupils in the class, you know. I used to get five shillings a day every day from my father as pocket money, which was quite a lot in those days and I used to have to pay it out to the class, a shilling to the toughest boy in the class not to get beaten up, sixpence to the chap who brought the football to school that day so that I could get a game of football, sixpence for a chap to sit next to me, and so forth. And sixpence to various geezers not to call me names and so on. Well, at the end of paying out all this, I'd end up with about sixpence for myself, and so it would

continue, term in, term out. You see, really I was in no position
to fight or rebel, because I was so hopelessly outnumbered.

G.J.: How many other black children were in the classes then or
in that school?

M.: There were no other coloured kids in the school until 1957.
Two years I spent there as a loner, a black one at that. Well,
really I learnt quite a lot there, you know, sort of growing up
with white people from the infant stages. I have learnt how to
more or less live amongst them and retain your sanity and, just
live along in general, you know. It calls for brains, not brute force.

G.J.: What were the reactions of your parents, or did they not
know of your having to pay for your security and safekeeping in
school?

M.: Oh well, they knew it all right, but there was really very little
they could do about it. My father just used to advise me to try
and learn as much as possible and as soon as possible he would
try to take me away from the school and the local environment
which I was in. Funnily enough, I remember one afternoon I
had a fight with one chap in the school and at half past three
when the infants go home his mother was waiting outside and
he told his mother, and his mother spat in my face, and I went
home and told my father about it and my father came to school
the next day and complained to the headmaster, and the headmaster said 'I think this is completely ridiculous.' I was probably
telling lies or a bit frustrated, so therefore I made it up. It was
quite unlikely that a parent or an adult of any description would
spit on an infant, especially a little coloured one who was so
affectionately liked throughout the school and the community.
Well, I tried my very best to butt in and interrupt him and tell
my father the facts, and each time I was subdued by the headmaster or a member of the staff who said 'Oh you naughty boy,
why do you tell such horrible lies?' Well, in the end they dismissed it as a figment of my imagination, or at least that's what
they tried to brainwash my father into believing. Well, since
then, from that day onwards, I started carrying a piece of glass

in my jacket pocket to school with me, broken glass, you know.

G.J.: How old were you then?

M.: Six years old. I used it a couple of times, I was threatened with expulsion, so my father removed me from that school and sent me to another in 1957, the end of July 1957. So from what I've just said you can see that really as the immigrant in those days, anything was possible, or anything could be done to you that was possible or that was detrimental to you, the black person, and be talked about as more or less fantasy in your mind because you were so hopelessly outnumbered, and when all the members of staff got together and said, oh what a nice boy you were and nobody would want to do that, who would disbelieve them against you. So I was made out to be a liar and a very selfish and spoilt little pupil. So that went down in my school record as well, and various pressures were also brought to bear upon me by the education committee for the offences I had committed of cutting up several other pupils.

G.J.: What were these pressures, what form did they take?

M.: They took the form that I would be sent to reform school where the bad boys were sent, where I wouldn't have to come out to play and all this. Sort of all the things that didn't appeal to a youngster at those times, you know.

G.J.: Were you taken into juvenile court, or were your parents summoned to court because of these cuttings?

M.: No, no, no, they weren't. They were more or less hushed up. My parents knew very little about what was going on, and when they were summoned they were brainwashed into believing the complete opposite to whatever had happened.

G.J.: Did they at any time blame you for what was going on, or did they accept your stories, or did they accept the stories of the school?

M.: Well in the early days my father used to accept the stories of the school, but after a while he realized that I was telling the truth and made everything possible at home to sort of compensate for the kind of pressures I was undergoing at school, such as buying train sets and everything I really wanted.

G.J.: Was he at that time, or was he and your mother at that time under pressure themselves in the community as black people?

M.: Well, 95 per cent of the community liked them, 5 per cent didn't, the 5 per cent that didn't were more or less Irish people. You see, up until the time the black immigrants started coming to this country the Irish immigrants were the persecuted minority in the community by the whites, and when blacks came over the Irish jumped at the opportunity to have someone on a lower rung of the ladder in the social scale to persecute, and so therefore throw off some of the burden off their backs on to the immigrants, so when I say 5 per cent I mean the Irish, who didn't really like us.

G.J.: Your father then decided to do what as a result of the way you were treated at school and the fact that it was difficult for you to exist there and learn under normal conditions?

M.: Oh well, my father was going to send me to prep school, but I cried and complained and I didn't want to go, because I thought to myself, the evil which you know is better than the one which you don't know. And whenever I wandered out of the normal playing area at home I was stared at and looked at, and I felt very strange, you know sort of more or less like a curio, like some object from outer space. So having got used to being stared at around the area where I lived I would rather stay there than go somewhere else where I had to start all over again. So in the end, 1961, my father took me to Shropshire to a boarding school, where I took an entrance exam, after having passed my eleven-plus at the junior school. How I passed it I don't know. I went to this boarding school where things were a bit different.

G.J.: Were there any other black children in the boarding school?

M.: Yes, there was one, a Ghanaian. His father was a chief or something, but he was more or less, he thought he was more or less a black white man, so myself and him didn't come into much contact during the school years.

G.J.: And how did you get on at boarding school?

M.: Well, boarding school to me was just a more intellectual sort of social community to what I had just come from, just more intellectual. Everything there that was directed towards me as racism was just done in a more subtle way, you know. Well fortunately, which I thank the Lord for every day, having the intelligence that I have I used to battle my way through quite well, and I managed to leave there with six 'O' Levels and one 'A' Level.

G.J.: How long did you stay in Shropshire?

M.: From 1961 till summer 1967.

G.J.: And then?

M.: Well, I went to a college of technology for a year, where I took 'O' Level Art and 'A' Level Geography.

G.J.: Did you visit home often from Shropshire?

M.: Oh yes, I came at half term and at the end of term.

G.J.: So you left Shropshire and came back to Handsworth as a teenager at eighteen. What did you do then, how did you fit in to what must have been a very new setting after your school years?

M.: When I left college I started joining once more with my old friends, all black, and we started going to the club. You know I used to go there before in the summer, but my parents didn't know about it. And I was quite shocked at the type of life which the other coloured chaps led there, I was completely shocked. It was more or less – like to me the first idea I got was that they were just a bunch of cut-throats, you know, I had wandered into some sort of tavern in the sixteenth century.

G.J.: Before you go on to tell me further about the club, which is where I met you, could you tell me what other forms of entertainment you had, whether you went to youth clubs and how you got into the groups you knew in the area before you went to boarding school, and generally how you fitted in to Handsworth again?

M.: Well, Steve and I were coming from more or less the same sort of social background, and having left boarding school, the year I was at college I never used to come out at night. I used to study quite a lot at home. And if I did come out I'd go to a club in town so I wasn't in any active form of social life in Handsworth at the time. In those days I still used to speak English wherever I went.

G.J.: English as opposed to what? What would you speak now?

M.: Oh well, Jamaican form of pidgin English which is more or less the English language cannibalized by Jamaicans, in a sort of parochial form that is in Jamaica, so this is the language which I have adopted at the moment because it's fairly quick and easy and everyone can understand it. It takes some of the pressure off your mind, in other words, it's for lazy people.

G.J.: And commenting further on the club, you went in there, you felt slightly out of place. How did that develop?

M.: I felt pretty green, you know, it's like you just stepped into a different dimension; to be serious, it is, in fact, this is reality. That place is like nowhere else on earth, specially in the twentieth century.

G.J.: Why is that so? What makes it so?

M.: Because it's so rum. It's the people that makes the club what it is more or less. They are from ages of about sixteen to, there's no limit from sixteen upwards as to the age group what go there.

G.J.: What would you say was the predominant age group?

M.: Mostly between seventeen and thirty, and out of this assortment you have narcotics sellers, you have pansies, you have thieves. . . . Well, a pansy is known as Percy in Handsworth, he's your ponce, living off immoral earnings.

G.J.: I thought 'pansying' was pickpocketing.

M.: No, they call that Jo.

G.J.: So pickpocketing is called Jo and living off immoral earnings is called Percy.

M.: Yes, so like a person'll say to you, 'You heard about Bill, he's just had five years for Percy.'

G.J.: So therefore it's a sort of 'in'-language, when you talk about Percy and talk about Jo people know what you're on about. What are the other characteristics of that group?

M.: Oh well, more or less the law is 'dog eat dog'. Each and every one of them tries to. I'll show you how they're so ignorant and stupid among themselves and greedy and avaricious. There are about six to seven permanent weed-sellers in the club, narcotics in general, right? Instead of them having a rota and saying, this week is for Tom and next week is for Dick and the next for Harry, and while they earn that week nobody else sells in there, we are making terms, right. No, everybody's there grabbing all at once, frequently a fight starts, you know.

G.J.: Fights? What causes those fights?

M.: Over clients, you know, as to who is selling the most weed. Among the sellers themselves and their friends. It can be quite a hellhole at times, you know. Amongst the Percies very little usually happens because they've got a code, a set code, it's very hard to get into that world, if you try to get in you're usually squeezed out unless you're some relative, or disposed of. After a few bashings you usually get the general idea that you're not wanted.

G.J.: And do people move away then?

M.: No, they usually turn to something else, either Jo or shooting narcotics, or becoming like Jeff, a predominant handbag snatcher, you know. It's interesting to know that one bloke went to gaol once, just by being searched in the Soho Road about two o'clock in the morning when he was found with four female lighters, and the officer said, 'Well young man, what are you doing with female lighters, were you thinking of handbag snatching?', and he made a blunder by saying that he hadn't snatched a bag in months, so they lashed him up. This was the first time that he went to gaol. Of course I think he's learnt his lesson by now. Oh yes, the last time he tried to fight his way out and ended up with five stitches in his head, from a police baton in the back of his cranium.

G.J.: These clientele, let's call them, at the club, the more regular members, or more regular customers, do they work or are the factors you mention their only source of existence?

M.: No, they have various forms of existence. The weed men sell to the Percies, the Percies are the biggest buyers of weed because without weed they can't get enough stimulation to do their necessary functions, right, because they are all sick in mind, they're more or less mental cases without certificates. Just by seeing the way they dress and their little mannerisms would give them away, if one is quick enough to see. Really I think the majority of them are living on borrowed time, and they don't realize this.

G.J.: What would you say was the build-up situation in terms of each individual within that setting? Why have these men become like this? Do you know their background?

M.: Yes, to sum it up quickly it's the fact that they have an inferior mentality, they are the true social misfits of the black immigrant community. They have no qualifications by which they may gain suitable employment, so therefore they know it is a disgrace to do labouring.

G.J.: They are discontented with unskilled employment are they?

M.: Exactly.

G.J.: And so they opt out?

M.: That's about it.

G.J.: How many of these men at the club do you think would want to get out of that setting?

M.: No, well, it has become a set way of life, they are too proud to admit to any stranger that they would rather live any other form of life than that which they lead, bar when it comes to serving their prison sentences.

G.J.: Do many of them go to prison?

M.: Every single one of them in the club has been to prison.

G.J.: For various offences?

M.: Percy, Jo, mostly. Snatching, grabbing and fling, you know.

G.J.: And they manage to live by this? – How many of them went to school in this country?

M.: Oh this is where it begins now. Most of them came here when they were over fourteen.

G.J.: And finished their education here?

M.: Most of them when they came here, like Kasa for example. Kasa came here when he was fourteen and he should have done one more year at school, but he didn't go to school that year, he spent it in Handsworth park playing cards when his parents thought he was at school. Playing cards, creating trouble, strapping the park keepers down and things like this.

G.J.: Playing cards for money?

M.: Yes.

G.J.: How many people would you say of that group in the club came to England at a tender age as you did and went to school in this country?

M.: None.

G.J.: How about Jack, shall we say?

M.: Oh yes, yes, but Jack's a completely different case . . .

G.J.: He continues to go there?

M.: Yes, now this is where I was trying to talk Jack out of it you see, because time is running out for him, you know. I keep telling him he should be going to college, at least to night school to try and gain some form of trade, learn something by which he may live off legitimate earnings eventually.

G.J.: What does he do during the day when he is not at the club?

M.: Sleep.

G.J.: So is it fair to generalize that most of the people who go to the club are nocturnal creatures?

M.: Exactly.

G.J.: They sleep during the day and go to the club in the evening, at night, and they operate at night, earnings-wise as well?

M.: Yes.

G.J.: To what extent do they come into contact with the police?

M.: Oh, it varies. Percies very rarely, weed-sellers, narcotic-shifters, I should say each of them about once every nine months and then they're away. The club is down to one quarter of its strength at the moment, did you know that? There's over thirty-five of the dining-room crowd in prison, serving sentences from six months to ten years.

G.J.: You mention the dining-room crowd, what makes them unique from the other customers in the club?

M.: They are the most violent group in the place and the most ignorant.

G.J.: And they generally congregate around the dining room?

M.: Yes, and in the passage. And every time there is a bulb put in the passage they smash it.

G.J.: What's the reaction of the gaffer, the manager of the club, towards them?

M.: Well, he would like to see every one of them dead or run over. Being in a very old and frail state there's not much he can contribute towards this, or the termination of their life on this earth.

G.J.: Does he not really depend on them for his custom?

M.: Oh well, if the bad element, meaning 99 per cent of the present regulars of the club, were to be ostracized from society or the community, then the workers would invade the place. You know, if it was quite safe for them to come with their wage packets without fear of them being stolen and fear of being battered and beaten, and having their wives taken away from them, they'd come.

G.J.: One thing one observes about the club is that on Thursday evening when a percentage of customers get paid and also Friday and Saturday evenings, the workers, let's call them, one sees many new faces in the club. During the week, before Thursday, Friday, Saturday, these people are at work, and they come there on Thursday, Friday, Saturday evenings when the pubs have closed. Is that a fair assessment?

M.: Yes, that's absolutely right.

G.J.: And so they are really fringe members of the club group?

M.: Yes, they're just as big, you know, mental degenerates as well, because they should have more sense than to come there. There are two out of five about every weekend beaten, battered and abused in some way or another by the crowd. You see the Percy men more or less keep themselves to themselves, you always find the Percies right up against the bar in the corner and they cause very little trouble. They spend most of their money in the club. All the trouble comes from the narcotics men, the Joes and the snatchers.

G.J.: Do the snatchers operate within the club as well as outside?

M.: Yes, they usually line the wall against the toilet area.

G.J.: And what if someone who has been snatched resisted?

M.: They usually get battered.

G.J.: What do you see as the future of these people in society in Handsworth today? To what extent have they opted out of what I am told is the discontent which is rising as a protest on the part of the total black community? Do they see themselves as part of this?

M.: Well they haven't got the mental understanding to realize their positions in the community bar that of total rejection.

G.J.: Are they aware that the police and the authorities generally are generalizing about Handsworth and black people in Handsworth because of the small crime element who they are?

M.: Well they realize that they are in the papers, the *Evening Mail* especially at night sometimes when they are being tried, but they haven't got enough sense to put two and two together. Otherwise they would at least organize themselves.

G.J.: Organize themselves in what way?

M.: In a more beneficial way to themselves, because right now it is, as I said before, dog eat dog.

G.J.: Dog eat dog which means . . . ?

M.: I'm all right, Jack, damn you. I mean, they can earn anything from £50 a week to £500 a week. They could have a little communal fund between themselves, just as weedmen or narcotics men, that when one goes to gaol they all put together and get a lawyer for him out of this communal fund and so forth, and have a rota for selling their drugs and what not, but they don't. Everyone distrusts each other.

G.J.: Is there generally speaking an element of fear and distrust among them?

M.: Yes.

G.J.: Do they keep personal friends?

M.: No, they won't trust friends, they won't trust anybody at all.

G.J.: They rent flats or rooms?

M.: Depending on their financial standing. Everyone in the club lives somewhere. One thing I can say for them, their houses and where they do live, their little section is very nice, you know. They really look after their house that way. Better than you would expect to find. But when they come to other people's place they try their best to destroy it. It's always in their mind you know, they are all each and every one of them dissatisfied with the way they are living, they're just too lazy to do something about it, or just too proud to ask anybody for help or for advice, or if they try to break away and they fail, to be laughed at by the rest of their community.

G.J.: If such help and advice were offered, how would it be received?

M.: With fear and distrust, because of their law of nature, nothing for nothing, which they have learned the hard way.

G.J.: So how then do you see this vicious circle being broken? You mention they could organize themselves in terms of common funds for these people when they are in trouble and that sort of community spirit among them, you don't see their organization for getting out of that rut, if you wish, as being in working and earning a wage and having decent accommodation for themselves? You don't think that's the sort of thing they'd go in for?

M.: No, no, no, no. Let us say, from the time when they've entered this country I know at least ten of the dining-room crowd who've been here over five years, from the time they were fifteen until the present day and they've never worked one day yet. They've been on the dole for the best part of three, maybe four years.

G.J.: How do they talk to the employment agencies, how do they manage to be on the dole for so long?

M.: By shifting their address frequently, learning off the older members of the game, and so forth.

G.J.: Do you, as one of the people who go to the club fairly regularly, do you see the social problem as regards the community in Handsworth generally?

M.: Yes, I'd like to see every single one of them eliminated because they are more or less just social parasites, well, no, I wouldn't call them parasites, each and every one of them.

G.J.: And would you like to see them eliminated?

M.: Yes, well as for the Percies, really they don't do much harm, you know, very little harm.

G.J.: Who do they trade with?

M.: Mostly Indians and white men. And they don't rob people, thieve or get themselves into petty rows, you see, because they know the penalty once they are found out, which is never less than five years, so they can't afford to mix with the weedmen. They go to the weedmen and buy five pounds worth of weed at a time and so the weedmen are really glad of their custom. So they are more or less a more sophisticated type of parasite.

G.J.: And do they in turn pay the women to work for them?

M.: Yes.

G.J.: And these women are Englishwomen?

M.: All white.

G.J.: Do any black women come to the club? One seems to see white women there predominantly, and very few black women, apart from those who work there.

M.: Well only degenerate black women will come to this place or those who are really misled, and they soon find out about it. They do know the environment, and decent women they come about once a month, with their husbands or boyfriends because of the lack of nowhere else to go.

G.J.: Are there black women who are on drugs or smoke pot or take narcotics?

M.: Oh yes, those who live with the Percies and the weed-sellers.

But they don't hustle themselves. They keep their women in the house and they have a smoke when he's having one.

G.J.: And do they work, these women?

M.: Depending on the ideas of the man which they live with. They're very rarely ill-treated, these black women, very rarely. The men have a great respect for coloured women, they never interfere with the West Indian women.

G.J.: To what extent would you say black youngsters, male and female, leaving home as a result of disagreements with their parents join the club group?

M.: Eventually about seven out of ten . . .

G.J.: Who get into that circle having broken with their parents?

M.: Yes.

G.J.: The papers, the *Evening Mail* in particular, speak of gangs in Handsworth. In your experience are there any organized crime agents, or organized gangs, in the accepted sense of the word, in the area?

M.: No, they are all freelance. Sometimes there might be two tonight, there might be three tomorrow, there might be four, there might be five, depending upon the occasion and what they choose to do, housebreaking or gallacing.

G.J.: What's gallacing?

M.: Well, it's just getting hold of an innocent citizen from behind and having a quick run through or gallace. It's generally white people, it's very rare they attack coloured people; either white or Pakistani.

G.J.: So the Pakistanis and Indians suffer the same fate as the white man at the hands of black men?

M.: Exactly.

G.J.: So in that sense there aren't any recognized gangs, but people who agree to work in groups for a special purpose at certain times?

M.: The worst time for the coloured youth in Handsworth is when he hasn't got his rent money, that is the most desperate black youngster you will find in the community. When Friday comes around and he hasn't got his rent money.

G.J.: What does he do then?

M.: On a Friday night when he hasn't got his rent money, the way he carries on?

G.J.: He is desperate and he goes through any measures to get it?

M.: Exactly.

G.J.: So once they organize themselves in groups of three, four or five and have done that thing, then they disintegrate again and act as individuals.

M.: Yes. Sometimes they choose different partners, there's a discrepancy over the share-out of the loot. Again, everyone distrusts everyone.

G.J.: So you can't at any time point to any particular group of individuals and call them 'a gang'?

M.: No, no, no, that's completely wrong. It's against their ethics of social warfare.

G.J.: How much of this does the police or the white community generally detect?

M.: About twenty-five per cent, which is usually the amateurs or youngsters just leaving school and entering the gallacing trade or Joey. The professionals, the older ones are very rarely detected.

G.J.: Is there a great code of secrecy among them?

M.: Yes. No one will give away anyone else unless. . . . You find the informers among the older group, there are no informers in the youngsters under twenty-five.

G.J.: And the older black men inform on people within . . .

M.: The black community. One informed on Jan; Jan was stuck away for five years. Jan had him chopped up.

G.J.: And he chopped up the informer?

M.: You know Drake, a pusher, you know, he's a recognized informer by one and all. From his face you'll see he's been battered and scarred. There's not much more can be done to him apart from death.

G.J.: This informer used to run the pusheen. And did the police not raid his pusheen because he was an informer?

M.: Exactly, yes. Moreover they supply him with drinks and so forth for information.

G.J.: Is that fact?

M.: That is fact. Very few people used to go there, only people who were strangers in town or white people, white hustlers from town, would go there because the coloured people knew what Drake was, so the only people who would go to Drake's – of the black ones were those who were totally immune to him, who Drake knew if he informed on them would get him shot immediately.

G.J.: Talking about getting shot and killed, do people have guns in Handsworth?

M.: All the Percy men have guns. All the higher forms of hustlers, and the continental weedmen. A pound of sarash sells for £1,000 in Sweden you see.

G.J.: They take it from England and go to Sweden to sell it?

M.: Those are the bigger men, the bigger fish. All those have guns and some form of armament.

G.J.: Do they carry them around with them?

M.: Yes.

G.J.: Apart from the club customers and the drug pedlars, the people who live on immoral earnings, the handbag snatchers and pickpockets generally, would you say there was a great crime among the rest of the black community?

M.: No, no, no, apart from the old law, that everyone get for themselves what they can get while bending the law to a certain extent, it all depends upon their position and how much they have to lose or how much they have to gain by turning to crime or illegal measures of earning their income.

G.J.: So when the police talk of crime in Handsworth, you think they are in fact talking of the same people recurring over and over again?

M.: Exactly. But they don't catch them.

G.J.: So in fact very few of them get caught?

M.: Very few. They usually pick on innocent youngsters and pin them with a lot of charges which these older crowd do themselves.

# 11. The white liberals who wanted to help

Institutional racism – manipulating the bureaucratic system to outflank the unwanted – may not be as rampant in Britain as in America, but it appears vividly among the planning and housing regulations. Black people often find it hard to secure planning permission for a building, particularly if it is for change of use, and it is peculiar how certain new blocks of flats in boroughs with a high proportion of blacks are populated by white, or nearly all white, families. Strange how roads like Curzon Road, in Brent, where the tenancies are in the control of the local council, begin to fill up with black people, while better class council accommodation 'isn't available' to them.

As an example of clear-cut institutional racism, the problems of the Handsworth Community Venture must take a lot of beating, if only for the reason that so-called 'important people' were backing it. As we have explained earlier, the Handsworth district of Birmingham is characterized by the worst features of the incipient British ghetto. It also stands out from most other areas of its type by the close proximity in which low-income blacks live to middle-and upper-middle class whites. Observing each other's standards of living at such intimacy causes bitter spoken and unspoken resentment. In some cases their gardens back on to one another, but they are rarely, if ever, next-door neighbours. Certain middle-class roads remain all-white, except for the occasional Asian doctor who is socially acceptable because of his medical status and good income.

On the brow of the hill near Handsworth park one can sense a frontier. It can also be seen with detailed observation. The whites have decided not to let the blacks come any closer to the more select area of Handsworth Wood and the fear of 'invasion' felt by the whites living close to the frontier is shattering to witness. Fear of falling house-prices is the most vocal complaint, backed up by grumbles about the blacks making a lot of noise, not tending their gardens, living in overcrowded homes, parking their cars in the road, children playing in the streets. One woman of around fifty and comfortably off included most of these complaints in her tirade and interspersed her talk three times with 'I have some very good friends who are coloured.' Another householder said: 'This is Harlem. You can't sell your home if you want to. We've got a lot to put up with and there's big support for Powell around here.' Nobody would give their names, saying they feared violent reprisals like a brick through the front window. The hatred is not only of the blacks but also of the Irish, of whom there are a good number in the district, indicating that their racism springs fundamentally from a fear of poor strangers who will drag down the level of the middle class environment.

In such an area it is inevitable that the black youngsters are jealous, bored and frustrated. They are outnumbering the white youth, who have mostly grown up and left the district to their parents. The five to fourteen-year-olds are helped by having a magnificent adventure playground between Hamstead Road and Welford Road, about 500 yards inside the frontier, which Bob Holman helps to run with a group of colleagues. The greater difficulties come with the teenagers, and gang rivalries give the police recurrent problems. Violence, knife fights and mindless vandalism break out sporadically from the youngsters whose energies are undirected.

Handsworth Community Venture was formed in 1968 to create a youth club which would combine a children's day-centre. Its patrons were the local members of parliament: Brian Walden (Labour, All Saints) and Sir Edward Boyle (Conservative, Handsworth). The executive committee included two Labour councillors, two Conservative councillors, a solicitor, a doctor, a teacher, a university lecturer and the wives of similar local worthies, all sincerely trying to do something to alleviate the problems which stared them in the face. As well as the two local MPs on the committee there were two local councillors, Mrs Muriel Locke (Conservative) and Mrs Sheila Wright (Labour). There were then only three blacks among the twenty-nine officers, trustees and committee, a deficiency which the Venture hoped to rectify when it had a base from which to run.

Officers of the Venture spotted a house in Wyecliffe Road at the end of 1968 which appeared ideal for their needs. It was a purely residential road but the house had been in multi-occupation as a boarding establishment for students. The asking price was £5,000. The road was not a white preserve; it had several black families but clearly some people, somewhere, had decided this was enough. The Venture put in an application to the Birmingham planning committee for change of use to a youth and day centre. A few weeks later they had a reply from the committee saying that after a circular letter had been sent to people in the Wyecliffe Road area telling them of the proposed youth club, there had been objections and therefore the committee could not grant the application. The Venture accepted this official rebuff with the equanimity typical of the middle class and resumed property hunting.

Premises large enough for community activities and at the right price rarely come on to the market in the area, and it was not until August 1969 that an alternative house was found. This was 180 Hamstead Road, within sight of the adventure playground. It is an ugly, red-brick Victorian home, three storeys high, and at that time needed a good deal of attention. In the same road – a fairly busy main thoroughfare – are a nursing home, a school and a few offices. The owner accepted the Venture's offer of £3,500, the completion of the deal being subject to a successful application for change of use from housing accommodation to youth club. The Venture's executive committee talked optimistically about having its first premises shortly and raised £1,000 among the membership. Sir Edward gave £1,000 from his own pocket. The balance of £1,500 was secured on loan. Already the members were talking about how the large cellar would make a superb discoteque which the young people could design and decorate themselves. Part of the building could be used as a clinic, some as a day-centre for mothers to leave their babies, with perhaps room for offices for social agencies.

But there was one horrendous snag. The side of Hamstead road on which the house stands is predominantly white-occupied. It is the same to the north. On the opposite side the roads leading off are almost entirely black-occupied. Number 180 was right on the frontier line, and certain elements of the white community decided that to allow a black community centre there was too much. Before the Venture could even put in a planning application to the Town Hall, a petition was circulating in surrounding streets opposing the project to change the house into a youth club. The idea came from none other than a member of the executive of the Venture, Councillor Mrs Muriel Locke. A doctor's wife living in a house just behind the proposed club said she wrote out the petition at the suggestion of Mrs Locke, who freely admits:

I encouraged the petition. I also opposed the purchase of the house at a committee meeting of the Venture. It was quite wrong to put it in a residential area and there were no parking facilities. We are trying to tidy up the area. The centre would have been used intensively. Why should we inflict this [asked what 'this' meant she explained: 'All the problems which may arise'] on hard-working people who have bought their homes and want to live in peace and quiet. I do not want them to spread further out. People can't sell their houses to prospective buyers. It would have been an explosive situation and I represent the views of the area. Anybody must feel incensed. People don't want to see their standards dropping.

Mrs Locke stressed when she said this that she was sympathetic to the Venture's getting premises – in the right place.

Opposition to the new centre had been conditioned by the erection of a West Indian evangelical church in Gibson Road, just round the corner. The whites speak bitterly of the noise which comes from the church as the hot gospellers get going. 'Their services don't last an hour like ours,' said one. 'They go on all day. You can't sit in your garden for the racket. Some conventions even last a week.' When the church was built a petition was drawn up by residents to block it, but it was organized too late. They were not going to be caught napping this time, thanks to Mrs Locke's tip-off. Frequent alarming reports in the newspapers of troubles among Handsworth's youth did not prick their consciences into a realization that a club might improve the district's reputation.

The petition against the club, signed by residents in four surrounding roads, was presented to the city council by another woman Conservative councillor, Mrs T. L. Walpole, and served as a blocking device so that the planning committee could not put the permission through formally – even if it had wanted to. The influential members of the Venture – and where do you find a more representative set of influential members in a community? – pulled strings for all they were worth to get the planning permission through. They were probably mistaken in trying the 'old-boy network' instead of organizing a counter-petition with more names. Some of the 'friends in high places' murmured nice things but added: 'Not in election year.'

The planning committee of the city council, which is Conservative-controlled, circularized residents in the vicinity of the proposed club, as it must do by law, asking for their views. The answers were not made public but, on the grounds of the petition and the answers, the application was rejected for four reasons: that it would adversely affect the amenities of occupiers in the vicinity by reason of noise and general disturbance; that parking could not be provided; it would interefere with the free flow of traffic; and that housing accommodation in the city was too scarce for these premises to be converted. There are 25,000 people on the housing waiting list. The city council, too, was sympathetic to the Venture's aims because it had voted £250 towards the project, but as Councillor Harold Edwards, the chairman of the planning committee, remarked: 'Residents had expressed their dislike for this particular use in that spot and under the 1969 Planning Act we must consider their viewpoint.' Yet, when one looks a little closer, one sees that three-quarters of the £250 which the council was giving was via the urban aid programme, i.e. the national taxpayer.

The Venture was furious. Sir Edward let it be known that he was deeply disappointed at the decision but otherwise maintained a discreet silence for although he had announced his decision not to contest Handsworth again for Parliament, he still wanted to continue his integrationist work until the general election without hardening attitudes by a public outburst. Mrs Locke was asked to resign from the Venture as her objectives did not seem in sympathy with the rest of the committee. That the siting of the proposed club in the 'right' place was the nub of the affair was underlined at a meeting of the city council. Councillor Mrs Wright asked: 'What type of property would the Venture have to acquire, and where, to obtain planning permission?' Councillor Edwards replied that he would like to meet the Venture's officers to discuss this. Councillor Edwards and Mrs Locke have since pointed out other places which they felt were suitable but the Venture has declined on the grounds of unsuitability or high price. More than a year after 'the frontier affair' it had still not started the youth club.

That we should see the Handsworth Community Venture story as a classic example of institutional racism is illustrated by two comments. Mr Bob Holman, who as well as running the adventure playground is Lecturer in Social Administration at Birmingham University, wrote in his book *Socially Deprived Families in Britain:*

The outstanding characteristic of Handsworth is extreme deprivation without any matching resources. On the other hand, an area like Sparkbrook, which by indicators of social deprivation stands relatively low in Birmingham, receives substantial extra local authority help, government priority help and generous contributions from voluntary bodies.

In simpler terms, if the Tories who run Birmingham pumped too much money into helping the blacks and the Irish in the Handsworth ghetto, then the white electors would vote them out. (All twelve councillors for the four Handsworth wards were Conservative at the time.) In other areas, like Sparkbrook, where the white vote is not so important, the councillors will spend money, albeit most of it from government grants via the urban aid programme and little from the rates.

The white liberals on the Venture received an education few

will forget. Mrs Pat Dickinson, a comfortably-off doctor's wife who at the time lived in Handsworth Wood and felt a genuine concern for the blacks down the road, says with an admirable frankness:

What I was dumb enough to think was a social problem is really a political problem. The immigrants feel they are battering against a fixed society. Doesn't our failure prove it? If do-gooders with our connections can't achieve things, what's the hope for them?

# 12. A long fight in search of justice

The police in the Notting Hill area of London have a bad name among the black people, however much they may deny that it is justified. Move among the people in this miserable, decaying district and the stories of police harassment and unfairness are legion. We could relate many, but we have chosen the story of Roland Ifill for two reasons: 1. it is a clearly defined case of policemen selecting a black boy for arrest when, even if he were guilty, nearly 100 other wrongdoers were involved; 2. it demonstrates that no matter how much skill, money and influence go into attempting to get a redress, none is likely to be forthcoming.

Roland was fourteen in 1969 and, like most kids of that age, football crazy. So much so that he joined the staff of Queens Park Rangers football club as a crowd steward, for which he received £1 5s. a week. He could walk to the Loftus Road ground from his home in Ladbroke Grove, which is in the heart of the black quarter. After helping to supervise the crowds through the turnstiles and running messages for the controllers, Roland was free to watch the game. He was proud of the armband which denoted his capacity as a club steward.

On 11 January 1969 there was a 'local derby' match between Rangers and another London club, West Ham United. There were probably nearly as many 'Hammers' supporters among the crowd as there were home team enthusiasts. Both teams are based in tough areas and have a proportion of hooligans among their following, and at this time violence and vandalism at soccer matches was prevalent in many parts of Britain. During the half-time interval a squabble broke out on one of the terraces between rival fans after insults had been hurled about different players' conduct and qualities.

Suddenly a gulf appeared in the crowd at one point; then it closed and about 100 teenage fans came to blows with their fists and feet. Roland and a friend, Robert Marti, who had used their knowledge of the ground to get close to the half-way line, one of the best vantage points, found themselves in the middle of the battle. Robert was kicked on the leg and Roland struck in the face. Neither struck back, but Roland put up his hands to cover his face – a perfectly natural reaction but apparently enough to make him a marked person by the two policemen who were bearing down on the fracas. Trying to escape the violence, Roland ran between the two struggling groups, who stopped the moment the police were spotted. Before Roland could get away he was seized by the police. Strangely, no one else was arrested. Oddly, no one can remember seeing another black person in the vicinity at the time.

Roland was then 5 ft 5 ins. tall and weighed about nine stones. He is a diabetic. Policemen make mistakes like everyone else, but what followed was inexcusable. Witnesses to the incident say Roland was handled very roughly by the policemen. One put his arm round his neck while the other seized his legs and lifted them up. They carried him horizontally to the low wall separating the crowd from the pitch and pushed him over. A former deputy prison governor, Douglas Gibson, who watched the whole incident, said afterwards:

> The policeman used excessive and quite unnecessary force on this boy who had not participated in the fighting, and kept his arm around the boy's neck far longer than was necessary. The other policeman also assisted in dragging him away. A spectator near me shouted 'you have got the wrong chap'. I consider the policeman's action to have been both unnecessary and unduly severe. I was very upset to see the police behave so violently in this matter.

A woman secretary, Suzette Hannagan, described the same actions, commenting, 'the behaviour of the two policemen throughout the whole proceedings seemed to me unnecessarily aggressive and intimidating.' Another witness, David Harvey, a building company director, spoke of 'unnecessary and excessive force'. He said:

The policemen slammed the youth to the wall and held him by his neck to the wall for a quite unnecessarily long period. One of the policemen had his arm pressed against the youth's throat and the boy appeared terrified. The policemen then lifted the boy over the wall head first and his limbs appeared to be going in all directions. He never tried to break away from the police. I was appalled.

Once over the wall, and standing up at last, Roland tried to explain to his captors that they had made a mistake but no notice was taken. Witnesses feel fairly certain that the police should have heard some of the cries from the crowd that the boy was innocent. Roland alleges that at this point one of the policemen said to him: 'Open your mouth and I'll slap your black face.' At this, already shattered mentally and bruised physically, Roland gave up protesting and was led from the ground by the coat collar.

Once outside, he was released. 'One said something to the effect that he ought to really arrest me,' says Roland, who walked along the road for three or four yards and heard a policeman say from a patrol van, 'Bring him in.' So Roland was re-arrested, put in the van and taken to Shepherds Bush police station. In the van Roland claims that one of the two men who captured him said, 'I don't like you black herberts,' and accused him of being the leader of the Winkie gang. When Roland again tried to explain that he was not, he says that one of the policemen shouted: 'I'll put my hand across your black face.'

We have only Roland's word for these racial slurs but the facts of the fight and the manner of the arrest are attested by reliable witnesses in signed statements. This was due to the public spirit of a barrister-businessman, Neville Vincent, who was sitting in the stand at the match and was so horrified at what he had seen that he took the names and addresses of a few of the people present in case they were needed.

His hunch was correct, because Roland was in deep trouble. He was kept at Shepherds Bush police station for several hours, missing a scheduled insulin injection meanwhile, and arrived home in the evening with a form from F Division of the Metropolitan police force indicating that he had been accused under

'Section 5 of the Public Order Act, 1936, as amended by the Race Relations Act, 1965, section 7.' The reference to the Race Relations Act was rather ironic.

Next day Mr Vincent, a director of Bovis Holdings, a large building and contracting company, wrote to the police asking to be informed if the boy was to appear in court. A few days later Chief Inspector Thompson telephoned to say that the boy was due to appear in Marylebone juvenile court. Mr Vincent went to the hearing ready to defend it – he had arranged a solicitor and witnesses – but the police asked for an adjournment so that they could also be represented by a solicitor. When the case against Roland was heard – he was accused of threatening behaviour whereby a breach of the peace was occasioned – the two policemen told their story, and three witnesses for the defence described what they had seen. Roland was acquitted but the lady chairman of the juvenile panel commented that there was no criticism at all of the action taken by the two police officers, who had to perform a difficult duty in an awkward situation.

Roland had secured justice but there can be no doubt that if Mr Vincent had not organized his defence things would have been different. The evidence of the two policemen was that Roland had been fighting, but the defence witnesses had shown that they were probably mistaken. Alone, Roland was poorly placed to get himself out of the predicament: at the time he was attending a school for maladjusted children. And as he had been in trouble before, a serious penalty could have been imposed. This previous case did not involve violence.

You might be forgiven for thinking that was the end of the matter. In fact it was only half the story, perhaps the least important half. If he had been born of middle- or upper-class parents who could feel aggrieved enough at the slight on their son to take action, he could have brought civil proceedings, through a parent, for wrongful arrest or assault. But Roland's father, from Barbados, works for British Rail as a guard and there is a large family. While the family were deeply upset at Roland's experiences they did not feel bold or rich enough to challenge the police through civil court proceedings.

Chief Inspector Thompson telephoned Roland's solicitor just after the acquittal and asked whether civil proceedings were likely. An assurance was given in writing that no action would follow so long as appropriate disciplinary action would be taken against the officers. Chief Inspector Thompson took statements from all the known witnesses and pursued his own inquiries.

A letter from the police commissioner dated 3 April 1969 was the next thing to be heard. It said:

Following a careful inquiry into the matter, a full report was sent to the Director of Public Prosecutions in compliance with Section 49 of the Police Act, 1964. The Director has now advised that he does not consider that there is evidence to justify any criminal proceedings against the officers concerned. This decision does not, of course, debar Master Ifill from taking proceedings (through a parent) if this course of action is desired. I am to add that the Commissioner is unable to find that the officers, in arresting Roland Ifill, acted otherwise than in accordance with their duty.

That last sentence was like 'holding a red rag to a bull' where Mr Vincent was concerned. How could the commissioner suggest the policemen had been acting in accordance with their duty in the light of what four independent witnesses to the incident had said? So began a battle by correspondence, newspaper campaign and parliamentary influence which lasted for more than a year. The cuts and thrusts of the participants are all a matter of record instead of the usual hazy recollection. No money, effort or string-pulling was spared by those who took up the cudgels on Roland's behalf. And Mr Vincent, who is a member of Justice, the all-party group of lawyers dedicated to upholding the principles of justice and the right to fair trial, is a doughty fighter who knows all the moves. Roland had everything going for him, or so it seemed.

The criticisms raised in recent years of the manner in which police investigate complaints against themselves would fill several chapters of this book. The relevant point to this – and many other stories – is that the evidence taken during disciplinary proceedings is never made public. Only senior police chiefs and the staff of the Director of Public Prosecutions see it. Sometimes the Home

Secretary or one of his deputies reads the evidence if a reply has to be made to a probing Member of Parliament.

Police Constables 208F Leonard John Bobbett and 478F William Anthony Doherty gave their side of the story of how they arrested Roland. There are, of course, two sides to every story and we would like to know theirs. But we are not allowed to. In thousands of cases all the public know is the perfunctory letter which arrives saying there is no cause for action, like the one Mr Vincent received. Occasionally, if a newspaper or an MP is persistent, some scraps of evidence come out in letters or statements but never sufficiently to be able to make a balanced assessment of the rights of a case. They are secret inquiries.

Despite this practice, Mr Vincent wrote back to the police commissioner making several barbed points, and asking whether any other evidence, other than that given at the court, had come to light which had prompted his decision.

You will appreciate [he told the commissioner] that the only interpretation which I could put on your observation that the police officers acted in accordance with their duty is that you (unlike the learned magistrates) do not accept the statements given by the independent witnesses, as I feel you cannot possibly think the police force is acting in accordance with its duty by arresting and charging the wrong person.

Three weeks later an assistant commissioner wrote back to say that the commissioner had studied the transcript of the court case.

The Commissioner is aware of the observations made by the learned chairman, from which he notes that she agreed that there was no criticism at all of the action taken by the two officers who had to perform a difficult duty in an awkward situation.

Then the letter writer let the cat out of the bag:

During the course of the inquiry [he wrote] statements were obtained from other officers and two independent witnesses (to the arrest and the fight which had preceded it) who had not given evidence in court. Their account of the incident supports that given by the officers concerned.

This admission that there were more witnesses available for the

rosecution than were produced in court raised two very im-
ortant questions: 1. that the police case could have been more
ffectively presented, and perhaps Roland found guilty. (The
Metropolitan police in particular like relying on the evidence of
heir own officers to secure a conviction, and so readily and over-
whelming are they believed by the magistrates that at the height
f the blacks–police confrontation in August 1970 in Holloway
nd Notting Hill, Mr Jeff Crawford, secretary of the West Indian
tanding conference, remarked – many felt with some justifica-
ion – that black people regarded the courts 'as a protection
acket for the police'.) 2. Why could not the complainants know
what the other side of the case was, and perhaps ask relevant
uestions on particular points?

Mr Vincent wrote angrily to the commissioner:

No opportunity has been given to cross-examine them [the new wit-
esses] and you have ruled on this issue without any kind of proper
nquiry, and without having had the benefit of testing which of the wit-
esses is speaking the truth. I am astonished to learn that other police
fficers witnessed this incident, and even more surprised that the Court
was not given the benefit of their evidence. You will appreciate that the
ublic is naturally concerned that someone like yourself, who is not an
ndependent body, should make a ruling on matters affecting the con-
uct of the police. And in this instance a clear imputation is being made
n respect of the veracity of witnesses for the defence. There is no room
ere for mistake, so it is clear that someone is not speaking the truth,
nd I once again ask you to have an independent inquiry set up so that
he evidence of all concerned can be properly tested.

Bit by bit the way the investigation had been carried out (and
here was nothing unusual about it) was emerging. An assistant
ommissioner explained in another letter:

The two private witnesses were traced after the Court hearing in the
ourse of the investigation and statements were obtained from a num-
er of officers who, although unable to give evidence regarding the
atter which was the subject of the charge against Master Ifill, were
ble to speak as to events subsequent to this arrest which were, of
ourse, relevant to part of the complaint.

he letter added that the commissioner still felt that the officers concerned in making the arrest acted in good faith and in accordance with their duty. 'The fact that the Commissioner came to this conclusion is, of course, no reflection upon any of the witnesses who gave evidence for the defence at court,' the letter ended tactfully. In effect, the letter writer was saying that the police were sticking to their story despite the other witnesses.

Mr Vincent challenged the police to let him have copies of the statements of the 'new' witnesses and expressed surprise that two private witnesses could be found so many weeks after the event. He was told that section forty-nine of the Police Act 1964, under which the complaint was dealt with, did not provide for the cross-examination of witnesses. Statute was not cited as the reason for not showing Mr Vincent copies of the 'new' witnesses' statements. A letter said:

It is regretted that it would be contrary to normal policy to supply copies of statements of the two private witnesses and of the police officers. Finally, I am to add that the Commissioner is of the opinion that his senior officer dealt with this matter completely impartially and that no further inquiries are necessary.

But an account of the case appeared in the *Sunday Times* on 6 July 1969, which threw up a fact which had not previously been noticed. The report said:

Mr Vincent's allegation against the police was investigated by Chief Inspector R. G. Thompson, of F Division. A Metropolitan Police spokesman told the *Sunday Times* that 'a chief inspector of a division other than that of the accused officers carried out the inquiry'. But Chief Inspector Thompson is based at Shepherds Bush police station – where Roland was taken – and documents in the possession of Roland's parents show he was accused by officers of the Chief Inspector's F Division. The spokesman said it was not policy to reveal the names of investigating officers but when it was put to Chief Inspector Thompson that he had conducted the inquiry, and the men were in his own division, he answered 'yes'.

An embarrassed silence fell on the affair until a letter appeared in *The Times* on 26 August 1969, from Mr Eldon Griffiths, Conservative MP for Bury St Edmunds, and at the time parliamentary adviser to the Police Federation. The letter said: 'it is a myth that the police are judge and jury in their own case'. He detailed how a member of the public with a grievance against the police could seek redress, and in point three of his letter stated:

All complaints are investigated by a senior officer who must have no interest, personal or official, in the case before him, and who is drawn from a separate division, and frequently a different force, from that of the accused man. Senior police officers carry out these inquiries for one very simple reason: they alone have the necessary training to do a thorough job, in the public interest.

Chief Inspector Thompson, based at Shepherds Bush, had had charge of the Ifill case since before the boy's first court appearance – it was he who telephoned Mr Vincent to say there was to be a hearing – and had conducted the entire inquiry.

The day after Mr Griffiths had seemingly laid down official police policy in his letter to *The Times*, a letter left the Home Office to go to Mr George Rogers, then Labour M P for North Kensington, who had taken up the case on Roland's behalf. Whether it was a coincidence that this letter went the day after *The Times* letter appeared we do not know. It may well have been, but the letter from Mr Elystan Morgan, then an under secretary at the Home Office, nevertheless contained the remarkable statement:

We have been disturbed to find that the investigation of the complaints made by Mr Vincent and others was carried out by an officer from the same station as the officers whose actions were the subject of complaint. The Home Secretary is therefore asking the Commissioner to arrange for a completely fresh investigation which will be carried out by a senior officer having no connection with that station. I will let you know the outcome as soon as possible.

You ask for an independent inquiry, but on the information we have at present neither the Home Secretary nor I think that this would be appropriate. You will know that the procedure laid down in section 49 of the Police Act, 1964, for investigating complaints is based on the recommendations of the Royal Commission on the Police. Cases have been brought to notice, through complaints, in which an independent inquiry under section 32 of the Act has been established. But these are highly exceptional and the Home Secretary feels he would be misusing his powers and undermining the established procedure if he brought about an investigation in the present case under powers other than section 49.

In concluding that no wider investigation should be undertaken for the present the Home Secretary is influenced by the consideration that examination and cross-examination about events which took place on 11 January is not likely to be very profitable – perhaps least of all to the boy who is at the centre of the controversy.

A police officer (when we asked who we were told we were not allowed to know) did conduct a second investigation into the Ifill affair. His identity has not slipped out but we have no reason to doubt that, with the Home Secretary taking an interest in the affair, it was an officer from another division. This officer did not even talk to Roland! At this stage Mr Vincent pressed the MP to try to get an investigation into how it should ever have arisen that an officer of the same station as the officers who were the subject matter of the complaint carried out the original inquiry. This, he argued, was contrary to Regulation two of the police (discipline) regulations, 1965.

It was February 1970 before Mr Vincent and the MP heard from the Home Office. It gave more details of the disciplinary proceedings. After setting out the early history of the affair a letter, again from Mr Elystan Morgan, said:

The two arresting officers identified by Roland Ifill gave statements. The first said he had seen the boy fighting and thereby causing annoyance to other spectators. He had led him by the arm to the wall surrounding the pitch; but the boy had struggled and he and a third officer, whom he does not know and cannot identify, helped Roland Ifill over the wall. He and the second officer then led the boy by the arm round the track and out of the ground. He has denied assaulting the boy and has declared that he only used such force as was needed to restrain him and stop him from escaping. He is emphatic that he did not put his arm round the boy's neck and hold him against the wall. The second officer identified by Roland Ifill substantiated this account.

Statements were taken from five other constables who had been in the vicinity, and they all said there was no undue violence; a police inspector who was off duty amongst the spectators made the same statement. Two other spectators made statements to the effect that

Roland Ifill had been actively involved in the fight at the football match and that no violence was used towards the boy by the police. The report of the investigation was sent to the Director of Public Prosecutions who advised that, having regard to the conflicting evidence, the prospect of conviction was not sufficient to justify criminal proceedings against the police officers. For the same reason disciplinary proceedings were not brought against the officers by the Commissioner of Police.

The second investigation was made by a senior CID officer from New Scotland Yard. This officer got in touch with a number of other witnesses by obtaining details from the football club of season-ticket holders in the stand in question, and by arranging for a notice to be put in successive programmes requesting witnesses to come forward. The great majority of those who came forward had no more than a hazy recollection of what had happened; some of them said that if there had been any violence they would have remembered it. Only one was able to give some support to the complaint made against the police on the other hand several spectators said that undue force had not been used. Apart from this difference on a point of subjective treatment, there is some conflict of evidence on whether the boy was struggling and the police had some difficulty in getting him over the wall and on whether the policeman at any time held the boy's head under his arm.

There is also some confusion as to how many police officers went into the crowd at the time. The fresh investigation has shown that at least one officer – a detective constable – helped the two arresting officers; but other men on duty and some spectators recall two only, whereas the two arresting officers recall another officer whom they did not know, but who was not the detective constable I have mentioned. The Commissioner tells me that there were a number of incidents that day, some of which were in the same vicinity. The two constables chiefly concerned in this case had arrested a youth in the crowd some 50 minutes previously and it is possible that some of the contradictions in the statements arise from confusion between incidents, as well as from inability to recollect exactly what happened so long ago.

The report of the second investigation was sent to the Director of Public Prosecutions, who replied that the further investigation had disclosed no evidence to cause him to alter his previous recommendation. In these circumstances the Commissioner does not feel that disciplinary proceedings would be warranted. I am disappointed that it has not been possible to resolve the substantial conflict of evidence, even on matters of circumstance, but I am bound to conclude that we are not likely at this date to elicit anything further which would be of value to us.

The second investigation had thrown up some puzzling features, not the least being the policeman who helped his colleagues but whom they did not know. One other witness supported the case against the police but his name was not revealed. Six other policemen – one an off-duty inspector – were found who could give evidence for their colleagues, and their loyalty is to be admired.

The tenacious Mr Vincent still kept up the attack. It struck him as extraordinary that of the new witnesses who were apparently present, no names had been given, and even more extraordinary that the police did not bring them to court to support their case. But what kept him most on his mettle was the complete absence from the last Home Office missive of the reasons for the second inquiry. He also pointed out that the *Sunday Times* had been misled by a spokesman who claimed that an officer from another division had conducted the first inquiry.

At the end of May Mr Elystan Morgan replied again:

I agree it could have assisted the judicial proceedings if the additional evidence recently provided by other witnesses had been available to the court, but at the time the prosecution considered that they had adequate evidence to bring before the court and, as you know, the additional evidence was obtained only after the investigating officer had interviewed about 100 persons.

He said that it was 'not normal practice' for the identities of witnesses to be disclosed publicly. But more surprisingly, the letter went on to say that the police can legally investigate a complaint against one of their own division – a shock for Mr Eldon Griffiths!

The relevant paragraph of Mr Elystan Morgan's letter says:

As regards the first investigation, this was not, as suggested, utterly contrary to regulation two of the Police (Regulations) 1965 which is applied in substance to the Metropolitan Police by their general orders. This regulation provides that an investigation should not be carried out by an officer serving in the same division or branch as the officer but it goes on to provide that *this should not apply where the chief constable directs that it shall not apply* [authors' italics]. Because of the size of the force, authority to exercise this discretion is delegated to subordinate command in the Metropolitan police, and as I explained in my letter of 27 August 1969, the Commissioner subsequently agreed that it would have been better in the circumstances of the allegations made in the Ifill case for the investigation to have been carried out by an officer from another station. This led him to initiate a fresh investigation.

Concerning the mis-information given to the *Sunday Times*, the Home Office accepted the commissioner's explanation that this was

an error arising from the fact that there is another officer serving at another station with the same name and rank as the officer in charge of the first investigation and this gave rise to a misunderstanding, but there was no intention to mislead.

The case had now been in dispute for fourteen months. The police tactics of making it so protracted a struggle that the parties lose hope would not have worked with Mr Vincent but for the fact that in the next month a general election was called. A new government took office and Mr Rogers, MP for North Kensington for twenty-five years, retired from Parliament. There seemed to be no point in continuing the fight.

The incident related here may be typical of others in its early stages but is extremely untypical in the manner of its pursuance. Because it was fought by a wealthy barrister with ample secretarial facilities, supported later by an influential Sunday newspaper, and a Member of Parliament, it might reasonably have been expected to have achieved a degree of success. But, despite all their know-how, they completely failed, other than getting Roland's original acquittal.

While it is true that the three parties to some extent used Roland's case as a vehicle for their campaign to alter the rules under which grievances against the police are examined, the boy was surely entitled to some redress. Even Sir John Waldron, the Metropolitan police commissioner, revealed in July 1969 in the *Job*, Scotland Yard's own journal, that he could see reform coming:

I am sympathetic to the idea of recourse to independent assessment of those complaints which are not the subject of criminal or disciplinary proceedings and in respect of which the complainant is dissatisfied with the outcome.

But Sir John also said that he could not readily see how this could be done in practice, and this was no doubt being looked at by the proper authorities. He went on:

Many of the arguments about the way we handle complaints centre around the fact that it is simply not possible for a police force to investigate in a fair and impartial way a case that involves the force. Widely reported instances have given rise to the suspicion that we cover our tracks, evade the issue, and generally set out to look after our own. Nothing could be further from the truth, yet the suspicion does exist, and we have to accept that we have a responsibility to allay that suspicion. I am determined to do everything I can to ensure the citizens' confidence in the force and that the morale of the force shall not be allowed to suffer just because we allowed ourselves to get stuck in an unyielding position on this whole issue of complaints against officers. Don't forget that the great majority of complaints against policemen stem from a failure in human relations. No one has ever pretended that policemen are not human. We are not perfect either.

The police advisory board has been working for some time on the issue of reform of the complaints procedure. If and when suggestions come, will they be found acceptable? The chief inspector of constabulary, Sir Eric St Johnston, in his 1969 report hinted strongly that any change would not be welcome, using the old argument that police morale would be put at risk. But the number of complaints is mounting: those in London went up from 2,924 in 1968 to 3,296 in 1969 (253 found substantiated) and in England and Wales from 6,357 to 7,351 (988 substantiated).

Complaints against police come from both black and white citizens but we find that some of the strongest protests about the manner in which the police look into complaints stem from black people. It is a source of grievance which could and ought to be eliminated swiftly in a sophisticated democracy such as Britain, in the interests of harmony. Throughout all the stages of the Ifill case – from his acquittal in February 1969 to the final, rather backtracking letter from the Home Office in May 1970 – no one in authority ever apologized to Roland. No one expressed regret at his suffering. The police commissioner wrote of his doubts about some part of the procedure and that policemen are 'not perfect either' but a diplomatic apology in the early stages might have saved the protracted wrangle. Yet nobody wanted to unbend. Roland, we trust, will not join the bands of disillusioned young blacks because, despite his powerful friend Mr Vincent, he could not beat the system.

# 13. The birth of a Black Panther

What America has today, Britain so often copies tomorrow. Militant blacks here might have borrowed the insignia 'Black Panther' and some of its tactics from the US political movement, but the motivation and aims of the British movement are original and sincere. With its powerful appeal to the young, Black Pantherism is growing in this country and it would be a mistake to think, as many do, that only West Indian immigrants and their offspring join the movement. A fair number of Asians are observable at Panther meetings.

Yet perhaps the most important feature is the number of racially mixed people who find themselves drawn to the militants. The extreme difficulty in getting racially mixed babies adopted into homes is only one sign that the 'half-caste' is still the 'whipping boy' of the European races. On close acquaintance racially mixed people can often be seen to have extraordinarily keen and sophisticated minds, and their physical beauty is often devastating if it can be seen through unprejudiced eyes. The hostility they are prone to meet in the course of their lives because of their unusualness and lack of conformity can make them the most racially conscious and thus extremely militant against those whom they believe are looking down upon them. If you ask such a person what colour does he or she regard themself the answer is more and more an uncompromising declaration of 'I'm black.'

While the Black Panther movement and similar groups in Britain are still new, inexperienced, poorly organized and small in following, they are nevertheless gaining ground. Both the authors of this book have looked at the Panthers fairly closely, in quite separate circumstances and, of course, from widely differing positions of race, upbringing and occupation. Neither has detected a wish for ugly, aggressive violence, which is associated with the Panthers in the public mind here, as a result of the tragic clashes between their movement and the police in the USA. Black militants here declare that, like the animal whose name they have adopted, they are peace-loving until attacked. Retaliation would follow.

A man who is probably the leading Panther in Britain at present told us:

> We do not preach or talk violence. We want to prevent violence against us. Our programme for liberation consists of demonstrations, protests and demands. But if there should be a confrontation here, as in the USA, with direct physical violence against us, we should not encourage our people to be pacifist.

This Brother (Panthers do not use Mr and Mrs but Brother and Sister because, not unnaturally, as the descendants of slaves they find the prefixes Master and Mistress historically odious) would not allow us to name him for two reasons: fear of being marked out by the Special Branch of the police as someone important to watch; and the organization's desire to avoid the personality cult which frequent quotation in books and newspapers engenders.

To attempt an understanding of the Black Panthers we selected one young man and have traced not only the story of his life but that of his parents, feeling that the greatest injustice that is done to a person who has just committed some 'act against society' is to judge him merely on the stark facts of the demonstration he made or the angry blow he struck, instead of his entire social background. Our inquiry began when we came across this letter from prison:

Dear Les

> Was great to see you and the brothers again last Saturday. Trust you all got back safely. Still counting the days before I'll be out of here on parole. Many thanks for the books. I'm getting the brothers here to read them and be together too. 'All power to the young!' Try and get me some gum shields before you receive my next visiting order. I am still the champ at boxing. Really blowing their minds. Power brother!
>
> Love to you and the other brothers and sisters.
>
> Ken.

Ken was born nineteen years ago to Thomas and Mary Ferguson in a little village in Grenada in the West Indies, the last of four children. At his birth Mrs Ferguson was forty-two and her husband forty-four. Sarah, the only sister, was already twelve, Leslie the eldest boy, nine and Sylvan the younger boy, seven. The mother and father were dedicated, hard-working parents struggling against a harsh economic situation in their islands. The father was born in 1908 and left home at six to live with his god-mother, so that his mother could cope with a younger brother, her husband, and her father who was bedridden by a stroke. Young Thomas was given various chores at the home of his god-mother, who was the village baker. He had to collect wood for the oven and the leaves on which the dough was laid in the stone oven. When the bread and cakes were ready he had to deliver them to the local shops.

Between the ages of five and twelve he managed to have only six hours at school each week, so that at that tender age he had already spent virtually half his lifetime in work. Schooldays ended at twelve and he was given an axe to fell trees so that he could be the main provider of wood for the bakery oven. In 1925, at seventeen, he emigrated for the first time – Cuba needed workers for the sugar-cane harvest and paid eighty cents a ton of cane cut. He remained in Cuba from 1925 to 1929, returning to Grenada for yearly visits during the 'dull' season. His second emigration was in 1929 to Guyana where he was employed first cutting timber and then as a bauxite miner. Three years later he returned home and took up work as a sawyer and timber merchant. After two years he apprenticed himself to a firm of builders to learn carpentry, joinery, painting and interior decorating.

Thomas married Mary Hamilton in 1940 and a year later left for Trinidad to work at an American air base as a builder. He returned to Grenada in 1944 to find that work was even scarcer in wartime and left again the same year for Aruba, in the Dutch West Indies, where he was employed by the Lago oil company as a painter and interior decorator. He was back again in Grenada in 1950 with 3,500 dollars saved to build a new house for his family. In 1952 Ken was born into this new home. In 1955 Grenada's worst tropical hurricane in recorded history cost many lives, devastating homes and huge tracts of agricultural land. Mr and Mrs Ferguson's house escaped with minor damage but, like everyone else's, their long-term crops – nutmegs, cocoa, and bananas – were destroyed. But having just spent 4,000 dollars and with Sarah at secondary school and Leslie just starting grammar school, situations which in each case demanded paid tuition and board and travel expenses, Mr Ferguson could not afford to wait until the land produced crops again. Britain was suffering from a labour shortage and was inviting Commonwealth citizens to come to work. So in 1957 Mr Ferguson uprooted himself and set out for London. This was his fifth emigration. In London the labour exchange was satisfied with the proof of his qualifications and experience as a carpenter and painter and decorator, recommending him to several firms all of which Mr Ferguson visited, but none took him on. In five out of six firms Mr Ferguson noted allusions to his blackness. Then a friend employed by J. Lyons tea shops told him that one of the firm's cafés needed staff, and he started as a kitchen hand at £5 10s. a week.

Back in the West Indies, Sylvan started at secondary school in 1957 bringing additional financial commitments. Out of his £5 10s. Mr Ferguson was paying £1 10s. a week for rent, £1 for food and sending £10 every month to Mrs Ferguson. Out of her allowance she had to make a monthly repayment of the loan he had raised to pay his passage to England. By now some money was coming in from the sale of bananas and yams. This was Mr Ferguson's plight for the first two years, relieved by an accidental meeting with an old friend from Grenada who helped him to get a job at £10 a week at the American air base in High Wycombe, as a janitor.

His wife, Mary, who had struggled bravely to bring up the family despite the enforced long absences of her mate, was the eldest girl of four children. She was born in 1910, went to school from five to twelve, but as the eldest girl was burdened with most of the responsibility of bringing up the younger ones. She did the washing, cooking and cleaning while her mother worked in the fields. By the time Mary was sixteen her mother's health had failed and she became housebound for the next seven years until her death. Mary Hamilton had been the mother to one family, with all its attendant work-load and cares, well before she married Thomas to start her own family life. Economic circumstances dictated that she saw her husband for only a few years at a time between 1935, when they started courting, and 1961, when she joined her husband in Britain, but her determination to do her best for her children and stand by her man was never in doubt.

She had burning ambitions for her children and taught them a kitchen philosophy handed down through the generations from African folklore. The oral traditions sustained her and she diligently and righteously passed it on. She taught her children to be proud though poor, to love the family and relations and to be kind and deferential to their elders. She did not apologize for the fact that she expected her children to be men and women at an age – ten onwards – which is unthinkable in more developed societies. In typical West Indian fashion she dealt harshly with those misdemeanours of adolescence that later generations have learned to accept as part of growing up.

Into this disorientated family pattern Ken Ferguson was born and spent his first nine years. His early years were fairly characteristic of children of his age in that background – a life devoted to play and adventure. Even at six he preferred to be caned by his mother and enjoy his numerous escapades, rather than to submit to her strict discipline as his other brothers had done, and which Mrs Ferguson expected would be repeated. Ken enjoyed sport and loved construction games which could be followed by tearing to pieces whatever had been built. His school reports spoke of him as highly imaginative and creative with a penchant for leadership. Leslie left school in 1960 and immediately joined his father in Britain, leaving Ken with his mother, Sylvan – with whom he shared a love of long discussions but whom he thought was too much of a disciplinarian – and his sister Sarah who was by then working and living fourteen miles away. Ken showed a strong dislike of the helping around the house and fields which is such a vital part of the fragmented West Indian family way of life. Sylvan conformed, so the relationship between the two brothers deteriorated and Ken thought increasingly of Leslie over in England as his only real brother.

His dream of a reunion was realized in 1961, when Mrs Ferguson and he set out to join Mr Ferguson in London, leaving Sylvan at home to finish his studies and look after the house and land. Ken, now nine, and in a new country, had to start growing up with a father whom he had not seen for nearly four years. Ken found life in an overcrowded London house an unbearable constraint. He looked back on his old home as a mansion and his old surroundings a paradise by comparison, and was too young to understand the economic forces which compelled his parents to come to live in one of the world's largest cities. Until he became accustomed to the new district and found a circle of friends he depended very largely on Leslie's company and influence. A strong rapport was built up on the foundations of the old friendship back home. It was soon evident that Ken had identified with Leslie as a substitute father-figure. The failure to come any closer to his father wasn't helped by Mr Ferguson's having to work difficult shifts and long hours so that he saw little of his small son. Mr Ferguson had by now repaid the loans for the passage of his wife and Ken and he was saving frantically to buy his own house. The extra long hours at work meant that Mr Ferguson was a rather washed-out individual while at home and a person more likely to shout 'No' and 'Don't do that' at Ken rather than be tolerant or playful.

Ken interpreted his father's behaviour not as discipline but as bed temper or 'doing the moaney', and soon began to ignore his father completely. He started answering his father back and expected Leslie to defend him in the ensuing row. As a result Mr Ferguson became self-effacing and mute, feeling that he was unable to control the situation and that his wife and Leslie might be better able to cope. So a boy who happened to need a father more than most never had one. Mr Ferguson's decision to abandon his father's duties nevertheless left him with a deep sense of hurt and frustration, and he felt that none of the boys had appreciated how hard he had struggled all his life for their good.

Mrs Ferguson, now fifty years old, was also obliged to go out to work to keep pace with the rising cost of living and the more expensive demands of a growing family. She had very little time to see or reflect what was really happening to her family. The affluent society and culture into which she found herself catapulted from a rural peasant background brought with it adjustment problems which occupied a great part of her attention.

Ken was reasonably happy at school, where he met a number of black kids from back home. They gave him some of the support he desperately needed both in school and out of it. Within the friendship group he also found help with the difficulties of interpretation in the classroom and on the playground. His hobbies were stamp collecting and accumulating a giant pile of comics, which upset his mother who constantly nagged him to read library books. Often she would burn piles of the comics which she found in his room, not realizing he was leaving out the unwanted ones and hiding his favourites out of harm's way in an old mattress.

Ken moved up into secondary school with his friends and settled down well for the first two years. History and geography were his best subjects but he also showed a flair for essay writing. He won several medals for swimming and running and at the same time dropped stamp collecting for cycling. Eight pals formed a spontaneous cycling club and went on long rides to Chigwell, Epping Forest and Richmond Park. Any member of the circle of friends who was unable to get a cycle was provided with one by their construction of a machine from spare parts. The all-day cycle excursions had the unfortunate effect of annoying Mrs Ferguson at the week-ends, for Ken was rarely at home either to help with the household chores or to have the regular meals which she found it difficult to provide on working days. Sometimes he would arrive home too exhausted to work and too full of doughnuts or chips to eat the cooked meal waiting for him in the oven. Home for Ken soon became a place where one looked in occasionally to eat and sleep. As the end of schooldays approached the cycling craze gave way to music – blue beat, soul and reggae.

At this time a significant change came about in the composition of the circle of friends. From the junior school years onwards it had comprised both black and white kids but it was noticeable that towards the end of secondary schooling the white boys were either keeping to themselves or existing as a separate group while the black boys were knitting themselves more closely together. The new black group was developing a sense of solidarity and brotherhood. Each member of the group was prepared to stand by any other who needed support, which generally was in situations involving parents who needed to be told exactly what the group was getting up to, or who were not too prepared to allow the group to come to the home of a member to play records, sit and talk, or mend their bikes. It was a virile, raucous, fun-loving group. In the streets near their homes they would laugh and shout as they did acrobatic feats on their bikes and some black adults in the neighbourhood interpreted this as the unruliness of a lazy lot who never stayed at home to help their parents with anything. When the gang was multi-racial the white residents talked deprecatingly of 'those boys' or 'that noisy lot' but now it was 'those rowdy blacks' and 'Don't they realize people live around here', or 'Haven't they got bloody homes to go to'.

The occasions on which the police turned up in the street where the black boys were larking increased. Their reasons for coming was always, they said, to investigate complaints from householders about nuisance. Complaints from white residents direct to the parents of a transgressing boy were frequent and the substance of the grouse invariably the same: noise and swearwords. When such a complaint came to the Fergusons, Ken would get a massive rebuke from his father who had by then given him up as something of a waster. Mr Ferguson would shout: 'I don't want these white folks knocking at my door and getting uptight with me.' He must have sensed the worsening climate because he would often add: 'I've never had police come to my door so when you do get yourself in trouble tell them not to come here.' As his temper mounted he would add the advice: 'If all you have to live for is your mates then let them get you out of trouble.' Mrs Ferguson would interject that the boy must have some freedom and that his dad's belligerency didn't much make him want to stay at home. To this Mr Ferguson would counter: 'Even when I was not with you, you never had any such troubles with Leslie or Sylvan. What's so peculiar about Ken? I'm not one of those who say this is what England does to children. England can only do that to children who don't care in the first place.'

Ken's qualities of leadership, noted from his earliest school-days, were now getting him into trouble even more than the rest of the gang. Hostile observers easily picked him out as the head of the group and he secured a higher complaints ratio than any other. Under this sort of pressure the group stopped frequenting the streets and took to the parks and open spaces. Very soon, to the park-keepers the appearance of ten or fourteen young blacks on bikes and carrying a football were synonymous with trouble. Many times the boys did stupid and wild things but some complaints also came from officious little men who enjoyed 'keeping the blacks in their place'. When the boys were in the wrong they scarpered but when they felt they were being wrongly accused they would stand their ground and a bruising argument would follow, which usually ended in a call by the park-keeper to the police for help.

The police began to watch the parks as assiduously as they had patrolled the streets. The story is the same from every member of the group: that having left one park and gone to another they could expect the cops to turn up there. As a result of this 'warfare' the boys began appearing in the courts on charges ranging from obstructing the public footpath, obstructing a police officer, creating a disturbance, to carrying an offensive weapon. The weapons were either a penknife, a screwdriver or a spanner. Ken appeared in juvenile court several times for relatively minor offences through making himself vulnerable by arguing with the police. Partly because they considered the offences trivial but mostly because the boys hesitated to explain to their parents about the circumstances which led to their arrest, the parents all too readily assumed the police were right. Parents went to court reluctantly, never engaged a solicitor for their son's defence, and hoped the punishment would teach their son a lesson and he wouldn't be in trouble again.

All too often the parent agreed with the police officer who called at the door and suggested their son plead guilty because it's only a minor offence and he would get off with a small fine if he pleaded guilty'. To Ken and his mates the dice appeared to be loaded against them. Even in such relatively small matters the alienation grew because both the police and their parents seemed to be against them. It was a bandwagon process leading to polarization. The parents did not seem fully to realize that they were contributing to what, for their sons, was adding up to a long record of fines, ending up with more severe punishments such as periods of probation and visits to detention centres. The 'law and order' approach by the parents and the police was creating a delinquent subculture among the area's black youths.

When he left school Ken was found a job in a garage by the Youth Employment Service. He was deeply interested in motor engineering and at first enjoyed his work. He soon made the not unusual accusation by a youngster claiming that he was doing a man's job for a boy's wages. And the £6 a week he earned didn't go far towards the clothes, records and coffee bar expenses he needed to give his life meaning. His mother did not ask him for a contribution to the household budget and even packed a lunch box for him daily. Ken took the short-term view that his mates were well off earning £11 a week in unskilled job while he, an apprenticed mechanic, doing an equal amount of work, received £6. His brothers tried to argue that he would be better off ultimately but after only seven months of the apprenticeship he broke it. He was unemployed for a month while he searched for another job. Perhaps the person most angry at this move was his father who reminded Ken that at the age of forty-nine, in 1957, he had been earning only £5 10s. This argument meant nothing to Ken and the father-and-son relationship deteriorated drastically. Ken knew he could expect his dad to come home angry and ready for a barney every evening, so he was careful to be out of the house in time. His mother fretted and sensed the impending trouble. It came at 5 a.m. one Sunday morning. A policeman was at the front door to say that Ken was being held at the police station in connection with a stabbing incident. True to his threat,

Mr Ferguson wanted nothing to do with the matter. It happened at a time when Mrs Ferguson was too ill to leave the house, while Sylvan also dismissed it as being Ken's own affair, but Leslie went to the police station to see Ken, who had been one of a group who was present at the stabbing and himself took 2s. 6d. from the stabbed boy. The court put him on probation for two years. It was a white boy who had been stabbed and soon there were escalating black versus white confrontations in the streets. Ken felt that whenever the police came to an incident involving the conflicting groups that they assumed the black boys were at fault and always interviewed them in a biased way. At the slightest bit of back-chat the boys were arrested on a charge of insulting behaviour.

Suddenly Leslie, the hardworker of the family, also deeply interested in politics and current affairs, was made redundant by his firm. He had been nine years with them and felt he had given good service. He says that white workers whom he helped train as repair-engineers were invited to move with the firm from London to Eastbourne while he was merely told that his services were no longer required. Leslie was out of work for several months and it was while he was job-hunting that he came in contact with the Black Panthers. They offered to help him and he joined the movement. At that time he knew very little about their philosophy but the conviction that the Panthers were determined to help blacks who were 'up against it' came over strongly. Their programme of 'self help' answered a spiritual as well as a material need in him. Leslie spent his time talking to youngsters about their relationships with white groups and with the police and in the course of this Ken became deeply interested, spending hours debating with Leslie what the Panther organization could do for him. Ken joined the Panthers and was gratified to find that some of the members were as old as his parents: it was the first time he had found common ground with the senior generation.

The time they had previously spent on the streets, in fun-fairs and discoteques, was now spent reading, debating and trying to interpret their everyday lives to themselves and their parents. Unhappily the hostility between black and white youths in the area was mounting and events soon came to a head. Provocation by both sides led to two ugly incidents involving several woundings. On both occasions Ken was accused of malicious wounding and on both occasions black boys were charged while the white boys were allowed to go free. In the general mêlée of the second incident, a street fight involving some twelve youths, one black boy was kicked unconscious by white boys, Ken struck a white boy with an iron bar and cut his ear, and other boys received minor cuts and bruises. The white boys who provoked the incident – as a court later agreed – were called as prosecution witnesses while Ken defended a charge of malicious wounding.

The black boys told us that the policemen asked them during their inquiries into the incident whether they wished to prefer charges against the white boys. They had replied that it was a fight, both sides had received injuries, and that they were prepared to leave it at that. The police allegedly replied: 'O.K. Just as well. Because the others don't wish to take the matter further either.' But the police photographed the white boys' wounds and gathered evidence for a prosecution. As he was only half way through his two years' probation, Ken's new offence breached that and the jury found him guilty of wounding by using more force than that required for self-defence and he was given a Borstal sentence. Soon afterwards the following Letter to the Editor appeared in the *Guardian* on 20 May 1970, relating to Ken's case:

## White Justice?

Sir, – White justice, man? A time ago, when appearing occasionally 'in crime', one understood that the Crown would present the case fully and 'indifferently': the burden of proof being on the Crown. In a recent case, the youngest son, about 18 years, in a family of my personal friends, was tried and convicted for assault causing actual bodily harm on two occasions. The trial was at quarter sessions, the offences were committed in Acton, Middlesex, where the family lived, having come from Grenada, West Indies. In a case where racial prejudice was paramount, all the more would one suppose the need for the Crown to present, and to appear to present, the case fully and 'indifferently'.

The trouble in which the young man was involved on the first occasion, started in a youth club. Another young black man who was there called out 'Hello!' to a white young woman who also was there. She promptly replied 'F—k off!' to which the black youth replied in turn, using her charming expression. The girl's white boy friend then began an assault on the black youth: and so it all began. Neither of the two whites above was called by the Crown – Why? The evidence as to how the trouble started came from the Defence. The second occasion, on a later date and in a street, seemed to lead from the first. The Crown called three police officers. Their evidence appeared largely to be about how the accused (who came voluntarily) and his eldest brother behaved at the local police station: the relevance to either offence of assault causing actual bodily harm escaped one.

The accused's mother returned to Grenada, before the trial, in disgust with the police. There she will doubtless recount the events to all and sundry – 'white justice, you hear!' She has my sympathy. – Yours,

Peter Bucknill, QC,
*Queen Elizabeth Building,*
*The Temple, E.C.4*

The trouble he was already in did not deter Ken from joining the Panthers in two street demonstrations while on bail awaiting trial at the quarter sessions. The Panthers demonstrated outside the American Embassy in London in protest against the murder charge against Bobby Seale, chairman of the USA Black Panther party. Ken was arrested intervening when he saw a black girl being manhandled by a policeman. Altogether sixteen people were arrested. A fortnight later Ken again joined a Panther demonstration outside the American Embassy protesting about American commercial involvement in Trinidad which had just undergone a Black Power riot. Ken was arrested again. Leslie, who was marching with him, claims he heard a plain clothes detective say to two policemen: 'That one over there is Ken Ferguson. Grab him!' On both occasions Leslie intervened demanding to know why his brother was being arrested and was on each occasion himself arrested and charged with obstructing the police.

Now nineteen, Ken Ferguson is more a Panther than ever. He

quotes the situations in the street and the parks to illustrate his belief that the police recognize him as a leader and have tried to eliminate him. At present he is coping well with the Borstal spell, using it to train his mind, so he says, to channel his anger into constructive leadership once he is free again.

# 14. The spark that starts a riot

'Blackie bastards!' yelled Kenneth Horsfall at three young Indian men who were leaving a café a few minutes after midnight. 'Blackie bastards, keep quiet and go!' he repeated. Mohammed Rashid shouted at him to stop the abuse and then attacked with his fists.

This was the beginning of the incident which triggered off the most serious racial disturbances which have occurred so far in Britain. The date was 27 July 1969. Some people – mainly politicians and clergymen – declare that the disturbances were not in fact 'race riots' but had their origins in alcohol, the hot weather and weekend idleness. Not only do we think that these worthies are ducking their heads in sand but their well-trumpeted verdicts have meant that the facts of the conflicts have become blurred and, more important, the deeper issues largely ignored. We are able to write now on the basis of on-the-spot observations during the week of the unrest, extensive interviews in the subsequent eighteen months and from a study of the trials of the people involved.

Horsfall, a nineteen-year-old furniture packer, ran off to get help after exchanging blows with Rashid. A gang of white men rapidly left their homes and came down the hill to meet the Indians. How many there were is uncertain because witness's estimates varied. The trial judge in his summing-up put the number as 'anything from seven to fifteen'. They included men who like Horsfall had convictions for assault, and a professional boxer. There was a running battle but the Indians – who were three in number with a fourth in the background – were outnumbered and Bhupinder Singh drew a knife which he had taken from another participant, Dian Singh Ball, during a violent argument earlier in the café. It was the only knife among them but it had tragic consequences.

Seeing the knife flash, Horsfall made off to fight the other two Indians. Singh ran after him and buried the knife once into Horsfall's shoulder and once into his brain. He died in hospital at 2.20 a.m. The blood-letting stopped the fighting and the police arrested the three Indians in nearby streets within a few minutes. Singh, aged twenty-two, and Ball, aged twenty-one, were sentenced to life imprisonment for murder. Rashid, who was twenty-six, was acquitted of murder but found guilty of carrying an offensive weapon (Ball had taken it from Rashid and was himself relieved of it by Singh) and given an absolute discharge, as he had been in prison nearly six months awaiting trial.

The fight was a typical Saturday-night brawl between young hooligans who had taken too much to drink. The chief constable of Leeds in his annual report called it 'a fight between a group of immigrants and a group of local white residents', but it was not such a clearly cut black versus white affair as that. Within the white gang was a man of Indian descent called Sayed Afsor Ali, who later gave evidence for the prosecution at the murder trial, while the Indian men were in the company of white girls. The brawl undoubtedly had racial overtones but the most significant aspect is that two of the Indians were from another part of Leeds and one (Rashid) from Birmingham. The fight took place in the heart of the Burley area which has a high concentration of Indians and Pakistanis, but the local Asians were not involved. Most of the Asian residents who would have been likely to be out on the streets at that time on a Saturday night knew Kenneth Horsfall – his home was a hundred or so yards away – and of his weakness for racial baiting when drunk. They would almost certainly have ignored him. But the three involved in his death were strangers and in their drunken state retaliated first with fists, then with a knife when the second attack came from a group double and perhaps treble their number.

The events which followed that fight are of far greater significance. Kenneth Horsfall's death happened too late for it to be reported in the morning newspapers and as the following day was Sunday there were no evening newspapers. The incident did not warrant inclusion in radio and television news bulletins, particularly as the quick arrest of the Indians had made the matter sub judice. So it was left to word of mouth to spread accounts of the killing around Burley and into other parts of Leeds. Sunday was a fine, warm day, people were out in their gardens – if they had them – or sat on their doorsteps in the sunshine, all circumstances were conducive to a high circulation of gossip. The versions of how Horsfall died grew more exaggerated as they circulated – one account had it that it was a ritual killing and forty Pakistanis had danced a triumphal war dance around his dead body! To add to the emotional overtones, Horsfall was one of nine children in a well-known local family and he had been married just over five months.

When the public houses opened at noon the stories spread like wildfire and as they closed at the end of the lunch period violence was close. But it took another session of drinking that sultry evening for enough people to acquire courage to put their talk into action. Police checked all the pubs in Burley and could not find a single Asian. This forewarned them of the racial trouble which was brewing. Derek Hudson of the *Yorkshire Post* reported how he was standing in a bar in Burley that evening and a smartly dressed man about forty said as he passed: 'There seems to be enough of us here now. Where are you from?' When the pubs closed at 10.30 people began to gather in Woodsley Road quite near to the scene of the stabbing twenty-three hours earlier. There was talk of 'doing the Pakis' – throughout the whole affair everybody referred to the killers as Pakistanis instead of Indians. Rumour circulated in the crowd that coach-loads of people from other parts of Leeds were coming to help in a big retaliation against the Pakistanis. As the crowd began to move forward – it numbered between 800 and 1,000 strong – there were shouts of 'We want a riot' and one woman bawled: 'We are going to smash up the Pakistani houses.' Middle-aged women were prominent in the verbal viciousness.

The police tried to persuade people to go home but the mob surged on to the café in Hyde Park Road, from which the three

Indians had emerged when they encountered Kenneth Horsfall, and smashed its windows. The fronts of several other business premises owned by Indians and Pakistanis, including the Star Café, were also damaged. Kenneth Horsfall's father jumped onto a garden wall and said: 'It is me that is suffering. It is me that has to go to the funeral. I don't want to see anything like this and my son would not have liked to see it either.' No notice was taken of his appeal. Another man also addressed the crowd from a wall: 'I don't like black men either but let us go home.' The crowd swept down into Burley Lodge Road and any Pakistanis still on the street fled to the top of the hill and watched at a safe distance from behind walls. The others kept to the shelter of their homes. Stones and bottles were thrown at windows of houses which the mobsters thought had black owners but many of their targets were white-owned. A white Hillman Imp saloon parked in Burley Lodge Place, which the crowd believed belonged to a Pakistani, was overturned and set alight by eight men. In fact it belonged to a white resident. As firemen put out the blaze the cries of 'Let's get the Pakistanis' increased and police formed a human barricade to head off the mob. Nazi salutes were given and cries of 'Sieg Heil' as scuffles between the police and the crowd broke out. Four policemen were hurt making twenty-three arrests.

Several of the men who had helped Horsfall in his fight the previous night were among those arrested and charged with threatening behaviour. The anger of the white community began to turn from the Pakistanis to the police when it was realized that the police were protecting the immigrants. A police sergeant was asked: 'Why don't you black your face?' Then he was called a 'Paki-lover' and told: 'Get out of the way, it's not you we're after.' Some of the worst violence occurred when rioters tried to release men arrested by the police. The conduct of the police throughout the entire disturbances was exemplary despite considerable provocation and violence used against them. A few militants persisted in shouting 'Get the wogs' and 'Pakis go home', but by 1 a.m. the area was growing quiet. Fortunately the rumoured coach-loads of National Front men coming to support the white cause, and car-loads of Pakistanis from nearby Bradford to defend their fellow-countrymen, either did not materialize or were headed off by community leaders.

During that week there was a considerable tendency to blame the news media for fanning the troubles, and while this cannot be said for the Sunday troubles a case can be made out that the media were partially to blame for the troubles which flared up on the Monday night. But the full story should be noted: when the three Indians appeared to be remanded on the Monday morning the police and solicitors in the corridor of the magistrates' court decided beforehand to say something publicly about the racial climate in an attempt to take the heat out of the situation.

MR BARRINGTON BLACK (appearing for Bhupinder Singh) asked the deputy head of Leeds CID: 'Would you say there is a simmering volcano of racial disharmony on the verge of erupting in the area?'

Detective Superintendent James Fryer replied: 'I would not put it as strong as that, but it has caused some disquiet in the area.'

MR BLACK: 'Would you agree that what happened on Saturday night was as a result of someone, not necessarily the dead man, but someone in his company, making highly disparaging remarks to the accused Singh?'

SUPT FRYER: 'This has been said.'

MR BLACK: 'And until this happened Singh was going about his business in a normally peaceful way?'

SUPT FRYER: 'Yes.'

The whole attempt at 'cooling it' misfired because the *Yorkshire Evening Post*'s banner headlines a few hours later stated: '*Simmering racial disharmony*' in Leeds is denied. The newspaper reported verbatim the particular exchange between the two men, which they had staged with the best of intentions, but the 'simmering volcano of racial disharmony' phrase stuck in everyone's minds. Five months later Enoch Powell told the

Young Conservative Conference at Scarborough: 'But a solicitor there [Leeds] last year described one district as "a simmering volcano, on the verge of erupting".' Mr Powell, too, had read the solicitor's words as a statement of fact and not as a question.

On the Monday night about 500 people gathered at the same spot, chanting 'Wogs go home'. When the surge forward began police reinforcements rushed in but could not stop more bottles being thrown through the windows of two Pakistani cafés. Anybody who incited the crowd to 'get them' was quickly winkled out by the police. The situation threatened to get as bad as the previous evening when a West Indian driving a car down a nearby street accidentally knocked down a twenty-one-year-old white man. As the chief constable puts it: 'This accident was in no way connected with the disturbances but rumour that the knocking down was deliberate caused tensions to rise temporarily.' One rumour said a police car had driven straight at the man; another that a car full of Pakistanis had deliberately driven into him. Bottles were thrown at the car and the driver by four youths who were promptly arrested, making a total of twelve for the night. Derek Hudson, the *Yorkshire Post*'s reporter, again pointed out: 'As on the previous night there were ringleaders, men who scurried behind the thickest crowds, urging "Let's get them".' Known members of extreme right-wing groups were seen in the crowd. Leaflets calling for the repatriation of immigrants were passed round.

That was the end of the violent demonstrations, although on the Tuesday evening many people hung around expecting something to happen. By now the police had the area so heavily patrolled that nothing could be done openly without their knowing immediately. The Pakistani community, not a little bitter that the trouble had been brought upon them by Indians from another locality, were by now thoroughly frightened. Men on night shifts did not go to work for fear of what might happen to their families; thugs took a delight in making threats to Pakistani shopkeepers of 'You're next' just for the warped pleasure of seeing the owners hurriedly clear their stock from the windows. Some Pakistani families temporarily left the area to live with friends and did not return until the following week. At Kenneth Horsfall's funeral, however, which took place without incident, several Pakistanis and West Indians were among the 200 mourners.

Two other events occurred which made the disturbance noteworthy. A week later when three of the rioters asked for bail a coloured woman Justice of the Peace, Mrs Diane Phillips, happened to be sitting on the bench. The chairman of the magistrates, Mr Gilbert Parr, announced that she had 'not taken part in the deliberations over bail to avoid any possible impression of unfairness to the defence'. The defence solicitor jumped up to say that on behalf of all his colleagues 'we are sure that any decision made by Mrs Phillips in any case would be free from any prejudice. I would like to make that perfectly clear.' A controversy of national dimensions began when it was pointed out that if white magistrates decided the fate of both white and coloured people in racial cases, where was the fairness if coloured magistrates (there is approximately one in each big city) were excluded from such decisions? Mrs Phillips, a West Indian, appeared to have been caught off guard by the chairman's asking her to stand down for the next day. She said:

I am sure that Mr Parr meant only to maintain the interests of justice, but I will not agree to be excluded from any case in the future, racial or otherwise. Now I have had time to think about it, I think the exclusion was wrong, especially in view of the public reaction.

Later Mr Parr agreed that he had made an error of judgement in excluding Mrs Phillips, but in the eyes of the black population the case considerably dented the reputation of the courts for impartiality.

A bizarre sequel to the riots came a fortnight later with the burning down of the café in Hyde Park Road in which Bhupinder Singh and Dian Singh Ball spent their last hour of freedom for a long time to come, and which had been the object of missile throwing by the angry crowds. The owner, Mohammed Akram, one of the Pakistanis who had fled up the hill from the howling mob, paid £20 to an unemployed man to burn the place down, thinking that it would be attributed to the racial disturbances. Akram was overdrawn at the bank, business was bad, and he wanted the £4,000 insurance money. The arson was amateurish and Akram went to prison for three years.

The two nights of rioting were followed by the city's Establishment frantically issuing statements about its causes and nature, for, as the Recorder of Leeds said two months later when sentencing some of the rioters: 'In one night you brought nationwide shame and dishonour on a city which had hitherto enjoyed a fine record for racial tolerance.' The Reverend Malcolm Furness, chairman of Leeds community relations council (which had only just managed to persuade the city council to help pay for full-time officers but none had then been appointed), declared roundly that 'they were beer riots rather than race riots'. Trouble had not been expected in Burley because there was no evidence of problems and no great tension, he said. The chief constable agreed with him about the beer. The then Lord Mayor of Leeds, Alderman A. R. Bretherick, was even more specific. 'There is no racial problem in Leeds,' he said. In a front page leading article the *Yorkshire Evening Post* derided the leaders. The paper said:

We believe neither statement to be true. Drink is consumed daily and in most places without race riots. And there is a race problem in Leeds as there is in most communities. To blink the facts will not provide a solution. The Editor's post-bag confirms there is a strong anti-coloured feeling among some people. It is of long standing. The difference between Leeds and elsewhere is that this city has wide experience of integrating immigrants. This justifies optimism.

Burley's Roman Catholic priest thought outsiders had stirred things up. 'Up to now there have been very good race relations in the area,' he stated. Mr Merlyn Rees, Under Secretary of State with special responsibility for race relations in the Labour government, visited Leeds at the end of the week (he also sits as MP for one of the city's constituencies) and was a little more realistic than the others. 'I wouldn't regard the trouble as race riots, but race played a part,' he averred, seeming to want it both ways. 'I do not put the blame for the incidents entirely on drink,' he continued. 'I think we have got to face up to the fact that there is a proportion of people in this country who are anti-colour. What that proportion is is anybody's guess.'

Several immigrant leaders let it be known that they had seen the trouble coming. Mr Khan Chaudhry, chairman of Leeds Pakistani Muslim Association, said pressure on housing was the focal point of tension:

In areas where immigrants move in the house-prices go up: the sellers take advantage. Young white couples who want to stay in the area because they have family ties resent it because they often cannot afford the increased prices. With housing and with jobs and over-crowded schools, little by little the tensions build up.

Mr Chaudhry, who serves on the local international council and the Yorkshire conciliation committee of the Race Relations Board, was one of those who had been fighting the city council for some five years to have a community relations officer. He states:

We were told there was no need. The immigrants are 'as good as gold' we were told. What happened in Burley is a grim reminder to all decent people who say there is no problem. We must find a way to change the attitudes.

Only one person had publicly predicted the riots. In an article entitled 'Leeds Immigration: A Black Future' in Leeds University's *Union News* on 24 January 1969, Mrs Maureen Baker, leader of the city's Congress of Racial Equality, was quoted as saying:

There could be an uprising in Leeds within five years. It is the industrial cities of America that are rioting, not the South. If something like that happened here, Leeds would be the place for it to happen, not somewhere like Liverpool or Birmingham.

It happened sooner than expected even by Mrs Baker, a white woman with extensive involvement with the black community, and whose organization's influence in persuading the immigrant community to stay indoors during the riots has been praised by the chief constable. Why?

The white community in Burley felt it was vulnerable to a take-over by the blacks such as has virtually happened in Chapeltown, another Leeds district, and in parts of Bradford. They felt obliged to retaliate against the killing of one of their number by (they presumed) the local Pakistanis. It is a matter of regret that the news media, due to the timing, were unable to help destroy this illusion by publishing the names and addresses of the accused Indians soon enough. In Chapeltown and Bradford it is unlikely that the white population would have felt itself strong enough to fight back. By coincidence, in the same issues of the Yorkshire newspapers which were reporting the Burley troubles, there were accounts of a court case in which an Asian millhand at Bradford was charged with murdering a white man during an affray. This caused no riot. The reason lies in Burley's special problems.

Burley is made up of brown-brick, back-to-back and tiny gardened houses on the side of a hill between the university and the River Aire. It was built for the English working class and the signs that it is fighting to maintain its character are obvious. Its character was shrewdly summed up by Bryan Hartley, community development officer (young immigrants) of the National Association of Youth Clubs, a Yorkshireman who spent many months of 1969 in Burley arranging a multi-racial summer play project for children:

Everybody and everything has their place in the scheme of things. To an outsider the streets in the neighbourhood look the same and the houses identical but for the residents there is a wealth of variation and subtlety about the neighbourhood which is invisible to the naked eye. According to its occupant, each house has certain characteristics which make it the best house in the neighbourhood. Thus one house might be considered desirable because it is the first to catch the sun in the morning, another because it is the end of the row. Other streets are classified as either 'rough' or similar categories. This classification system is not based on fact: it is also entirely relative: each person has his own system of reference in which he can place his own house, his own street and the streets of the neighbourhood. And so, of necessity, because it is personal, no two people's systems are alike. It brings order and stability into his life. After living in the area, my most vivid impression was how well ordered life was. I felt that the pattern they impose helps to bring order out of anarchy and chaos and provides a framework into which the rest of the world can be slotted. Then came the immigrants: how could they be fitted into this highly stylized, conceptual scheme of things?

Asians have been living in Burley since the end of the 1950s and their numbers have been increasing. In 1964 Leeds was estimated to have 7,000 black immigrants, in 1967 it was 12,000 and currently about 15,000. Among these the Pakistanis have increased most in the last few years and total about 5,000. About a thousand Asian families live in Burley, as well as West Indians and Chinese. It is an extremely compact area and neighbours can observe each other's lives closely. One big complaint just before the disturbances was the story retailed around the pubs of the Indian who kept going to a shared toilet in his pyjamas. Most toilets in Burley are out of doors, many of which are approached by leaving the front door, down half a dozen steps, turn the corner and it's under the front door steps. We never heard that the Indian was indecently attired; just that it is not the done thing in Burley to wear night attire in the open air! If you are advertising a house for sale in Burley – and they often go for £400 or less, cash – then 'own toilet' is a big selling point. The local authority is modernizing as many houses as it can acquire – providing better bathroom accommodation, and whole blocks of irredeemable property are shortly to be bulldozed and redeveloped. As the quality of life in the area improves so will the race relations.

Burley is a hard drinking district, in the true Yorkshire tradition. But go into the public bars and you will see few Asians. West Indians love the English pub, with its darts and dominoes; Indians 'enjoy a drink', but Pakistanis, who are Muslims, do not touch alcohol. This is one thing which makes them a breed apart to the average Yorkshire working man who practically lives, especially at weekends, in his local. The Pakistanis work gruelling overtime hours in an effort to improve their material status, while at the same time sending remittances to poor relatives back home. A hunger for education quite outstanding for any race is obvious among the young Pakistanis. A survey in Burley, for instance, showed that 54 per cent of male school leavers had gone into further education.

Some stirring up had been done in this little patch of unrest. About a year before the 27 July riot the National Front distributed leaflets extensively in Burley, more thoroughly than any other district in Leeds. Burley has had a cell of the Oswald Mosley Union Movement since the 1930s, when Leeds was as notorious for its anti-semitic campaigns as the East End of London. The cell has blown hot and cold over the years according to the racial climate. But to blame the trouble on extreme right-wingers and outsiders is escapism; these people have a very keen perception of where their 'market' is and develop it accordingly. The chief constable rams home the point: 'Many of the persons arrested for disorder during those few days of disturbance had a previous history of disorderly behaviour and the majority were local residents.'

Burley had its two nights of shame because an area with a strong sense of white community saw the increasing arrival of the Asians as destroying their traditional way of life. This is precisely Enoch Powell's argument, but he is as mistaken as were the rioters, the East End of London's 'Paki-bashers' and others who denigrate the Pakistanis. There is a multitude of evidence on a personal, daily level, that Pakistanis are beginning to fit into our society. The field of education provides most indications. Our mills, factories and foundries need their labour: we must then accommodate them within our society. By the beginning of the Second World War, Leeds had taken in some 30,000 Jews from Europe. They were demonstrated against by thugs, fulminated against by demogogues, yet today are thoroughly integrated – and they have a distinctive religion like the Pakistanis.

# 15. The enemies of black people

In the last five years Britain has seen the renaissance and birth of organizations which are akin to the Ku Klux Klan and the John Birch Society in America in their unremitting hatred of black people, even if not in their violence. Rhodesia's illegal seizure of independence and the first Race Relations Act were their springboards in 1965, but Enoch Powell's speeches in 1968 brought an even greater surge of support for the older groups and created new ones.

It is an unwritten rule in British journalism to print as little as possible about extreme right-wing organizations because the publicity only helps them to recruit members. But in 1970 neo-Fascist groups began to come into the open to a far greater extent than previously. Was this because they felt a Conservative government would be less likely to prosecute? And cases came to our notice where ordinary people were duped by these organizations through lack of awareness of their true nature. Our research and observations reveal abundant evidence that some of the campaigns against the blacks are far more virulent, better organized and financed than were the Jew-baiting attempts, principally in Leeds and London, during the 1930s.

The activities of these insidious organizations must be brought into the open so that their philosophy and objectives are generally understood and they can, like the Ku Klux Klan in the USA, be stigmatized in the public consciousness.

The authors have been told that they are over-reacting to small groups of harmless cranks. Considering the racism evident in Britain today this is like saying that Adolf Hitler's Nazi Party meetings in the beer halls of Munich in the 1920s were unimportant. We do not equate Hitler's position then with the crazy extremists in Britain today but we do say that without their exposure to criticism, sarcasm and satire by British journalists and politicians they may prosper on fertile ground.

## The Monday Club

A group of businessmen in the Chelsea and Knightsbridge area of London who used to meet every Monday for lunch were so appalled at Conservative Prime Minister Harold Macmillan's 'wind of change' speech in 1961 predicting imminent emergence of new nations in Africa out of the dying British Empire, that they formed themselves into the Monday Club. Their object was to organize opposition to the 'pinkish' way the Conservative party was going. The club had no impact until 1965 when the white minority in Rhodesia seized independence illegally. The Monday Club backed it, calling for an end to trade sanctions by the UK against Ian Smith's régime. In 1968, the year Enoch Powell made his three anti-immigrant speeches, the membership increased by 90 per cent. It was more than 1,500 strong with branches all over the country and in the universities, announced the chairman, Mr Paul Williams, a former Conservative MP. The Club supported Mr Powell's views on race wholeheartedly even though this brought about the resignations of their founder, Mr Paul Bristol, and a patron, Lord Boyd of Merton, a former Conservative colonial secretary.

The most notorious Monday Club pamphlet was 'Who Goes Home?' by George K. Young, a former diplomat and banker, printed in 1969. He called for repatriation of Commonwealth immigrants and, like Powell, advocated a cabinet minister with responsibility for overseeing the return home programme. Money now going to developing countries in the form of aid should be diverted to the repatriation programme, he said.

Before the general election of June 1970, the Club had membership among thirteen Conservative MPs in the House of Commons and thirty-five members of the House of Lords. After the election it had thirty-one in the Commons, among them at least six in the government. Thirteen would not allow the Club to reveal their names. Its branches have tried – notably and without success at Surbiton and Worthing – to get Tory MPs with liberal views on race replaced by Powellites.

An indication of the sinister nature of the Monday Club came in a letter sent by its universities group to the Home Secretary about Herr Rudi Dutschke, the German former student leader, whose permission to remain in Britain was withdrawn. At the height of the controversy over whether Britain should allow Dutschke to study here, the group said that he had 'involved himself in political activities contrary to the conditions on which he was allowed to come to Britain'. A Club official declined to tell *The Times* (29 September 1970) how the evidence was obtained, adding:

> It is common knowledge in certain quarters but not necessarily the ones that I or journalists move in. I think it will be well known also at the Home Office. If needs be we can produce the evidence. At this stage we see no point.

## The National Front

Although the National Front was formed as recently as 1967, the experience of its leading members goes back forty years. The Front was formed from a merger of League of Empire Loyalists, famous for their dramatic and eccentric interruptions of political meetings in the 1950s and 1960s, the British National Party, which was anti-semitic and anti-immigrant, the Greater Britain Movement, which was neo-Nazi in its outlook, and the Racial Preservation Society, which is blatantly racist.

A. K. Chesterton, the Front's national director until 1970 is, as he never fails to point out, a nephew of the writer G. K. Chesterton. Now in his early seventies, he is a former member of the British Union of Fascists and a founder member of the League of Empire Loyalists. He spends his winters in South Africa. At the end of 1970 he resigned after an attempt to oust him by a militant wing of the Front who wanted a younger man with Powellite sympathies.

The Front thought of 'law and order' as a political gimmick

before Richard Nixon or the Conservative Party. It also wants 'to restore the issue and control of the national currency to the Crown', encourage home-ownership, stop the 'brain-drain'. Its aims and its literature are saturated with racism. Its ideal would be

to replace what is now known as 'The Commonwealth' by a modern British world system which, while ensuring the sovereign independence of each nation, would work for the closest cooperation between the UK, Australia, New Zealand, Canada and Rhodesia, and in which, if they so desired, the Republics of South Africa and Eire would each occupy an honoured place.

The Front adds a note that it would agree 'to permit the association with this new world system of approved Afro-Asian countries *on terms acceptable to its foundation members*' (the Front's italics). In the Front's manifesto it is stated that it would also be desirable

to preserve our British native stock in the United Kingdom, to prevent inter-racial strife such as is seen in the USA, and to eradicate race hatred by terminating non-white immigration, with humane and orderly repatriation of non-white immigrants (and their dependants) who have entered since the passing of the British Nationality Act, 1948.

While the Monday Club's strength lies mainly in the corridors of power, the National Front is financed and supported as a populist anti-immigrant movement. It pretends it is a high-minded organization interested in the Common Market issue and stiffer penalties for criminals, but its field work is almost entirely based on racial prejudice. The 'Stop Immigration' leaflet, full of errors and exaggerations, is sprayed out at public meetings and assiduously placed under thousands of windscreen wipers on parked cars. Eschewing violence, the Front seeks to create disharmony between blacks and whites by setting one off against another and trying to discredit the Race Relations Act. It publishes 'Candour' and 'Facts' and numerous leaflets like one on the Sharpeville massacre in South Africa in 1960. If the police had intended a massacre at Sharpeville, says the Front, then all 209 police officers, not seventy-three, would have opened fire on the Bantu. It describes the officer in charge of the police force which killed 69 blacks and wounded 180 in a matter of seconds without injury to themselves as 'a very brave man'.

The Front was wealthy enough to put up ten candidates for parliament at the June 1970 general election. All were in towns where they might be expected to profit from the white backlash, and all lost their £150 deposits. Only two – at Wolverhampton N.E. and Southall – got more than 1,500 votes. At the municipal elections a few months earlier the Front fielded many more candidates in multi-racial areas with greater success. At Huddersfield the Front contested thirteen out of the fifteen seats and came away with ten per cent of the vote. In Wolverhampton's St Peters Ward, where there was no Labour candidate, the Front's man got 753 votes to the Tory's 1,204.

'What Mr Powell has said does not vary at all from our views,' Mr Chesterton told *The Times* (24 April 1968). 'It is impossible to assimilate people of such differing racial stocks. You've only got to see the results in South Africa to know that it creates a most unhappy society.'

## Immigration Control Association

The most paranoid of all the anti-immigrant groups is the Immigration Control Association. This Association devotes considerable energy to a hate campaign against blacks. It boasts links with ten similar organizations, and was formed in June 1968, after the second Powell race speech. Among other literature, they distribute a

glossary of current political fictions propagated by our press and politicians to disguise the fact that we are being conquered by stealth under the misleading euphemism of 'Commonwealth immigration'.

The glossary describes the immigrant community as an 'alien occupation force' and racial integration as the 'imposition of coloured aliens on the defenceless native British'.

The weirdest of their definitions is that of the term multi-racialism as

an infamous experiment with human lives, utterly contrary to natural law and thus to divine order; in which the victims are for the most part the most defenceless in our community – the old, the sick, the poor, widows and spinsters living alone or with elderly parents, the school-children and mothers-in-confinement.

One of their leaflets, called 'The Great Betrayal: Facts on Immigration', contains such blatant untruths as there being 2¾ million 'coloured aliens' in Britain and that they have brought with them leprosy, a new form of TB, venereal disease, smallpox and typhoid in large quantities.

The Association gets demented about any extra cost which black communities may incur and wants the £362 million – a mysteriously computed figure – which it claims the immigrants are costing Britain diverted to a repatriation fund. It never refers to the fact that blacks pay income tax and that there are almost no black old-age pensioners. The Association cooperates with the National Front in stirring up friction between black and white communities and addresses meetings all over the country stressing 'low standards of hygiene which have caused great offence'; letters are written to newspapers in towns as far away and as white as Torquay, Devon, claiming that Moslems in Batley, Yorkshire, bury 'uncoffined bodies in cemetries despite objections'. The Association also helped with evidence for the defence of the five members of the Racial Preservation Society acquitted at Lewes Assizes, in 1968, of charges of inciting racial hatred.

Just how much damage is done to racial harmony by this Association, whose principal male supporter appears to be a Conservative Councillor in a London borough who alternates as chairman and vice-chairman, is hard to assess. Abusive racist language – 'our object is to rid our country of the whole tribe of uninvited and unwanted coloured aliens in our midst, constitut-ing a potential fifth column' – is unfortunately acceptable to many whites since Powell's outburst.

## Racial Preservation Society

The seaside resort of Brighton is the base of the Racial Preserva-tion Society. Formed in 1965 – the year the first Race Relations

Act was passed by parliament – it calls itself 'essentially an educational body and seeks by presenting the true facts of race within a rational framework to make some contribution to the humane solution of the race problems in the interests of all peoples'. This quotation is from Issue No. 5 of *Southern News*, the occasional newspaper of the R.P.S., which was the subject of charges against five members at Lewes Assizes in 1968 for inciting racial hatred. They were acquitted but not given costs. The defence called 'expert witnesses' who retailed doubtful scientific premises about the fecklessness of Negroes and the innate superior leadership qualities of whites. These went unchallenged by the prosecution who had not thought to call their own experts in rebuttal. The case opened up a loophole in the section of the Race Relations Act (Section 6) dealing with incitement to racial hatred: as long as racist literature is sent to members of an association it is within the law. Extreme right wingers have also boasted since the case that they learned a lot from it about how to write what they want and avoid prosecution.

The R.P.S. has two main targets: denigrating blacks and pouring scorn on white liberals.

Issue No. 7 of its paper said:

Five million coloured aliens now in Britain? We challenge the Government to prove that this figure is inaccurate! In May 1965 a police report to the Home Secretary stated that the Home Office figure of 800,000 coloured immigrants in Britain was a gross underestimate and that the figure of 2,000,000 would be more realistic. It was also stated that an estimated 750,000 immigrants had entered this country illegally! These estimates are based on an intensive nation-wide investigation into forged passports. Add to these figures the hundreds of thousands of coloured births and continued legal and illegal immigration and the total must be in the region of three million plus. *Unofficial estimates from observers throughout the country* [authors' italics] suggest that the figure might even be as high as 4½ or 5 millions.

There is no evidence that such a police report ever existed. The police are well aware that they are not equipped nor do they have a mandate to make population estimates. The story about illegal immigrants probably comes from the same source as it did to the authors: pub gossip by the odd racist policeman. The figure we heard was one million illegal entrants! Such a preposterous figure can only be believed by racists. At the time of writing the best estimates (which even Enoch Powell does not dispute) agree that about 1¼ million Commonwealth immigrants are now lawfully in Britain. During the second half of 1971 we shall know the results of the national census taken on 25 April 1971.

Other examples of R.P.S. sick thinking: 'Race mixing is a dirty and unnatural thing; it is against the will of God and means for Britain national suicide.' (See head of chapter.) In an article referring to monkeys receiving transfusions of human blood, an R.P.S. article says:

> So if blood is to be used as a yard-stick we can, perhaps, expect to hear demands for 'One monkey, one vote', a situation that would make the political situation in certain African countries even more chaotic than it is at present.

The R.P.S. delights in printing photographs and full addresses of the homes of people like Márk Bonham Carter, former chairman of the Race Relations Board and now chairman of the Community Relations Commission and Lord Boyle, the former Conservative MP for Handsworth, Birmingham, both notable champions of integration. After sneering at their large homes, R.P.S. invites 'You coloured chaps' to move in with Bonham Carter and Boyle in multi-occupation.

Some three million leaflets and broadsheets have been distributed, claims the R.P.S. It has also been host to two conferences of the Northern League, a European organization fostering the cult of racial purity, and it was at Brighton in 1969 that the 'Powell for Prime Minister' movement began. It is usual for members of the National Front, Immigration Control Association, Union Movement (a hangover from Sir Oswald Mosley), National Movement of St George and National Democratic Party also to be members or supporters of the Racial Preservation Society.

# 16. Why Black Power in Britain?

'Too little – too late' was the statement made to sum up Britain's efforts to meet the challenge of black immigrants and their descendants to this society. Talking about the social and political effects of immigration, a speaker on the subject of race suggested that Britain reacted to Commonwealth immigration no differently from the way it reacts to an unexpected and prolonged snow-fall; the moral of his story being that because Britain is never prepared it finds itself taking drastic, ill-advised action when it's already too late.

The philosophy of 'do nothing and wait – time, the great healer will cure all' bedevilled race relations in Britain for just under two decades. Many refused even to look for what needed to be cured. Bad housing? 'More white people than there are immigrants have been on local authority housing lists long before we were swarmed out by immigrants.' Better and brighter schools? 'Our schools have been dingy and overcrowded with our own poor kids for a long time. Ask the National Union of Teachers and they'd tell you how long they've been campaigning for smaller classes and better conditions.' Decent jobs? 'With so many of our own kind unemployed why should these blacks come here and demand the right to take our jobs? Some of them are even bold enough to refuse what they're given.' At the same time a new cliché was being coined, even by the experts:

Once they are born here and grow up in our society, go to our schools and (implicitly) do as we do; once those young ones coming over to join their parents mature in our society they would be all right and would help to build a perfectly integrated society.

The prophets sat back and pronounced, letting time run its course. For this if for no other reason many are now admitting, albeit reluctantly, that things are none too good for the second-generation 'immigrants' who being British-born are expecting more and better and are becoming mighty angry now they are not getting it.

Each black community in Britain, each area with a black population, has its percentage of British-born blacks and British-matured blacks who are busy defining themselves and working out their stance toward this society. Their platforms are numerous and varied; cafés, youth clubs, discoteques, parties, record shops, restaurants, playing-fields and the confines of their homes. The conversation that follows was recorded by one such group in a café:

One thing that bewilders and frightens most English people is the dress worn by greater numbers of black young men and women every day. We West Indians and Africans regard our dashikis, our boobas, broaches, pendants, beads, our curly hair as expressions of our belief in our blackness ...'

'A crucial stage in the position of black peoples throughout the world is the resurgence of our culture and redefinition of ourselves by ourselves. For us it's got to be a living process by which we say physically and psychologically: the white man's definition of me, a black man, has enslaved my body and mind. I believed his definition which said he was superior and I was inferior, lacking in intelligence, lazy lacking ambition, unable to take care of myself, ugly, broad-nosed, thick-lipped, over-sexed.'

'I believed the man, like the majority of us blacks. In order to be like him we had to try hard to be everything he was, even to become a lighter shade of brown rather than black. Back home most of our parents insisted we found a light-skinned, mulatto type girl or boy to marry. Because I'm black I could get a job at a bank or in government only after all the mulatto types had been placed. To be black was really to stay black.'

'Now we must be black both in mind and body. We must say for our own psychological satisfaction and self-respect: "We ain't going to hate ourselves any more, we ain't going to be self-effacing, self-denying any more. We ain't going ape the white man's standards of beauty, superiority, class any more. I no longer despise my blackness. What's more, I want to let it shine forth."'

'Our long black hair and imposing black beards, our colourful shirts and highly embroidered dresses, the necklaces and wooden figures cannot, must not be gimmicks. For the West Indians among us it must be part of a cultural heritage which the majority of us still relate to even if it's now almost totally lost to the West Indies.'

'Brothers, to the whites looking on even now what we're saying would sound like romantic fantasy and a load of idle talk. Just remember the British conservatism which now looks askance at us black creatures in this threateningly odd dress comes of the same stock as that which arrogantly demanded that whole nations in their own land change almost overnight and become subject to British rule, British tastes, dress, culture and religion. And yet they're the first to quote to you and me: When in Rome do as the Romans. When hundreds of our black brothers and sisters turn up at the Royal Garden or the Hilton Hotel in full evening dress, or when you see some of them walking round London with brolly, brief case and bowler, that is much more acceptable to white Britain than when we decide to have a massive carnival parade West Indian style round the streets of London.'

'Yes, and for many the paranoia goes even deeper than that. The police in particular seem to equate black consciousness with black militancy with black power; however they define that. Many of them assume like the rest of the British public that everyone with thick black hair and wearing a dashiki is a black extremist. It's a wretched situation in which you're undesirable because you're black and you're even more intolerable because as well as being black you're politically conscious and socially aware.'

'I would imagine by now most policemen and magistrates in black neighbourhoods know the shape of an African wooden comb and that like any other comb it's used for combing hair. Yet more and more our brothers are being picked up with these combs and charged with carrying an offensive weapon. And even when you point to your hair and tell the cops you use that comb because you couldn't possibly comb your hair with anything else they still don't believe you. Then the magistrates say things like: you would agree that this object is capable of inflicting quite a nasty injury if one wanted to use it for that purpose! I could say the same for the brollies people walk around with, but no one just picks them up for carrying offensive weapons.'

'Another thing is the hairnet some of the brothers use. Some brothers cut their hair and use the piece of stocking to put over their head to keep the hair in shape. Some use it because they just don't have the time to spend combing out their hair before they rush off to work. But many of the brothers get done for carrying that piece of stocking in their pockets because the cops think they go around stealing women's handbags and they use the piece of stocking as a mask over their face. When you try and explain the true use of the thing policemen jeer at you and magistrates laugh you out of court; at the same time warning you you're not so dumb as to fall for your unlikely story.

Here we are given the expressed feelings of young blacks working towards a concept of self, seeking to affirm a culture and having their symbols and the mode of expression misunderstood. They project something foreign, alien, and refuse to 'do as we do'. Second-generation blacks are sometimes referred to as 'the misplaced generation', and this not inaccurately: they are a generation of people who though British born are black and therefore suffer the same injustices and rejection from British society as their parents. Being neither British, West Indian nor Asian they are forced to evolve a culture which is peculiarly theirs. They relate to West Indian or Asian cultural patterns second hand. Their history begins with slavery, colonialism and post-colonial immigration. To this history, pages are still being written which speak of 'a dark menacing threat', 'send them back home [?]', 'they are responsible for half the crime in our cities', and as can be gathered from this book discrimination, poor education, poor employment prospects, denial of a sense of identity.

They are therefore attempting to find an identity, one which can only be black, not Asian, West Indian or British by nature. This entails an identification with and a search for black history, black heroes, black culture, black literature. Herein lies the basis for a true identity. Herein lie their roots. Though British born they are expected by white society to deny themselves, to accept second place and to be grateful for it; to accept the burden of the new modern-day post-colonial slavery in its liberal cloak, to accept the definition of blackness and of black people to which their forebears were expected to answer; expected to deny blackness if they are to be accepted by and in white society.

They are the new generation, not in whom the answer lies as the prophets predicted, but who are challenging society to help them find an answer, the answer that might help to determine the future of this society as far as their existence within it is concerned. Rather than make apologies for its blackness the new generation uses every opportunity to affirm it. It is of no small significance that their parents' generation reacts as negatively to Black Power in ideology and practice as do the majority of white people who feel threatened by it anyway. One often hears community leaders, social workers, police and black parents talk of unemployed black teenagers as 'easy prey for the Black Power boys'. This betrays both fear and misunderstanding of the notion of black power and an inability to see it as a direct response to the oppression, alienation and self-effacement of black people as a whole and in particular of the generation with which we are concerned. This misunderstanding is characterized at worst by empty talk about integration and at best by pointing to a few token blacks in positions of power and suggesting that given time their numbers would increase.

It is idle to talk about integration when so little concern is expressed about inequality. To integrate a people who are being made the scapegoats for the decay and deprivation in the areas they have inherited and who are made to bear the brunt of social inaction is to create a deeply entrenched group of disaffected, second class citizens.

The futility of flogging the integrationist horse cannot be overemphasized, and by the same token it emphasizes the point made earlier that the new generation are challenging society to help *them* find an answer, one which would help determine the future of this society *vis-à-vis* their existence within it. Part of what a deprived area is deprived of is self-respect, dignity, and the sense that ordinary people have some control over the shape and texture of their lives. Within this context the strategy for black people lies in working towards black consciousness, political organization for economic, social and political change. To many blacks these are still empty words. Many have come to depend on welfare paternalism and regard it as sacriligeous to attempt to have a say in the running of their lives. Many more possess colonial minds, the decolonization of which is part of the black struggle. The conditioning process by which black people learnt to hate themselves and distrust their fellows dies hard. Black consciousness asserts that there is no freedom without human dignity, self-respect and black peoples' belief in and acceptance of themselves and their black brothers. The divisive nature of self-hate which by promoting black consciousness black people hope to eliminate is that which makes the following possible:

'When a black person goes to a supermarket and buys goods he goes to the till and pays up without any fuss. Many, however, go to the corner shop of the black man and expect to come away with credit or with goods at half-price. If the grocer protests and demands his money he is immediately called a black capitalist bastard.'

'One black man had a grocery and provision store two doors up from an Indian store of the same kind. The West Indian originally had a good number of black customers. The Indian decreased the price of some of his goods and soon the West Indians were saying of the West Indian shop-owner: "Never trust black people. They too damn tief". While they all flocked to the Indian shop. Before long the West Indian shop-keeper folded up his business.'

Many small organizations pioneered by black people for black people spring up and fade out of existence every year. The leaders of such groups invariably affirm that they go out of existence because of lack of faith and trust in the organizers and support for their aims and objectives.

Political organization is viewed with pathological distrust by most adult immigrants. Many groups set up to give help and advice to the black community pride themselves for being non-political. This is reflected in the nature and constitution of the early immigrant organizations in Britain. These were generally acceptable not only because they were non-political but also because they depended largely on white liberal support. They started with artificially integrated committees and worked towards integration though most of their activities were concerned with apologizing for the blackness of the black man. Because this negative attitude to politics is still very prevalent Black Power, Black Self-determination, the Black Struggle still commands very little support among the majority of blacks. Black power is still being deliberated as though it is something yet to be achieved. In fact it is already there to be exercised but with neither the consciousness nor the political awareness to make it effective. This power lies as much with the thousands of blacks taking up their positions at work every day as with the black organized groups scattered around the country hoping to reach the black workers. But because these groups comprise for the most part the articulate and the educated as well as those who could afford the time, there is a danger of their becoming elitist in nature, using both a language and a method that is alien to the masses of people whose support they want.

Nevertheless this support must come even if the issue will continue to be diversified by token pieces of legislation or the efforts of workers in the race relations industry. The deprived experience their needs continuously and relate directly to every aspect of their deprivation. Yet they are never invited to participate in measures allegedly introduced to improve their conditions.

For many years black organizations have been trying to improve the conditions of black people on an almost exclusively parochial basis. None of those groups could be considered daring or politically challenging. They had to beg, they were expected to be deferential, they were dependent on white liberal support. In 1968 however there came the turning point in Britain. In the summer of 1967 Stokely Carmichael had visited Britain and spoken at The Congress Dialectics of Liberation at the Round House, Chalk Farm, London. He also visited various black communities and saw black groups in those communities. In 1968 the book *Black Power* by Carmichael and Hamilton appeared. The message brought by Carmichael to blacks in Britain and the framework presented in his book gave new life and purpose to numerous black groups in Britain striving as they were at the time to work out an ideology. Then as now the familiar warning against drawing comparisons between the

American experience and the British race scene was being presented. Carmichael pointed the way to Eldridge Cleaver, Bobby Seale and the US Black Panthers as well as to Frantz Fanon, Aimé Cesaire and other apostles of negritude whose works have influenced the philosophy and direction of the black movement in Britain. Also in 1968 race relations in Britain, already a growth industry, was nationalized.

Among the memorable events of that year are the passing of the Commonwealth Immigrants Act in February which limited to a trickle the number of East African Asians holding British passports who could enter Britain; the announcement in April of an allocation of £16 million for educational priority areas; the dismissal of Enoch Powell from the Conservative shadow cabinet on 21 April subsequent to his Birmingham speech advocating drastic stiffening of immigration policy; the passing of the Race Relations Act, which gave new strength to the Race Relations Board set up in 1965 and founded the Community Relations Commission.

It is important to look back over the two years since those momentous pieces of legislation and to ask whether they were meant to benefit the black man and improve his condition and if so to what extent they have succeeded.

On what basis for example were educational priority areas determined? The Community Relations Commission – 'Ethnic House' as it is so pointedly nicknamed – is another case in point. Despite black representation on all levels of this organization, how much could it be said to be tackling the real issues as far as the position of black peoples in this society is concerned? It is afraid of black militant challenge or participation. It is powerless and virtually ineffective not only because integration – harmonious community relations even when that involves fragmented accidental communities – is at once its starting point and its goal, but also because it fails to highlight the real issues as far as black people are concerned. What black people expect from the community relations commission is not patronage and a referral service or interpretation to the statutory agencies, but a plea on their behalf to local authority and central government,

a plea it could only present after careful examination and research. Black people expect the commission to present the sort of
data which is garnered (or ought to be) by community relations
officers during every day of their jobs, and which, hopefully,
would influence policy and legislation by ministries and departments of the central government. The C R C produces reports of
conferences on employment of black school leavers, on education
of black children, on youth work in a multi-racial society and on
similar subjects. One wonders to what use this information is
put. As if we needed reminding one senior official of the C R C
told us: 'Community relations officers are not black power
agitators or vanguards of the black cause. Their concern is for
the whole community, black and white alike.'

Like self-determination, participation in government by the
underprivileged and deprived is considered a crime. There are
many unwritten pieces of legislation outlawing this process. The
race relations industry gets through thousands of pounds every
year; the C R C alone manages to spend £400,000. Departments
to *study the immigrants* spring up like mushrooms, financed by
trusts and foundations. Yet the only relationship most of them
have with black groups is that of visitors to a zoo. Their findings
are never meant to enable the deprived to take action and very
rarely influence the government to shoulder its responsibility.
Money continues to be readily available to them while the black
groups whom they so like to study are afforded nothing even after
considerable begging.

If half the money expended annually by the industry was
channelled into the communities for them to help themselves
there might just be less need for 'experts'. But 'like the under-
developed countries from which they came they cannot be
trusted to run themselves. It is irresponsible to let power or
money fall into their hands, – i.e. it is forgivable to have experts
make mistakes and blow hundreds of thousands every year while
they plough on like ships without a rudder. It is inexcusable to
romanticize about self-help and self-determination and then not
to trust a black group to know what to do with £500. The hard
fact is that despite the various departments of the race relation

industry the black man continues to live daily with the knowledge that he is being confirmed more and more as a second-class citizen. Parents, themselves disillusioned and frustrated, see their children become misfits in an educational system and a home environment which enables them to do little more than 'tip-toe through society'. It is a serious situation when parents actually believe that they are somehow privileged because their children have been admitted to special schools to be given *special* treatment, failing to understand the true nature and purpose of the educationally sub-normal schools and schools for maladjusted children, into which more and more black kids are being admitted every day. It is equally serious when the reports of many children's departments year after year contain statements like: 'The number of mothers bringing children and leaving them with us saying they "just can't cope any more" causes us great concern.'

If black people, young and old, allow such children to be the sole responsibility of the children's departments, the ESN schools and their suspect tests employed in assessing the intelligence and potential of black kids, the probation service, the juvenile courts and the police, the schools as we know them and the youth employment and careers service after them – if the black community does not regard this situation as first and foremost its own individual and collective responsibility, then it tacitly gives assent to the denial of a life full of purpose and meaning to a high proportion of its own members. It virtually invites upon itself its own continued oppression and subjugation. Black people dare not expect power to be given. Where it already exists it must be exercised, where it does not exist it must be created. In working out a strategy – which black people can only do for themselves – the significance of the black labour force in this country cannot be overemphasized. The fact that the invariable response to the repatriation cry is to question what would happen to the health service, the transport service, the textile industry and so on, is proof in itself that black power is already a reality.

We feel that among other factors a lack of consciousness of the role society is prescribing for the black labour force of this country, i.e. a producer force without status and equality, militates against the possible dynamic use of this power. Until such time that the masses of black people become aware of their political potential, and that not only the few elitist groups possess the message but the people most qualified to sell the gospel, i.e. the workers themselves, black power as an ideology and a force to contend with, a real challenge to the policy-makers in this society, remains only a far-off goal yet to be realized.

As well as working to promote black consciousness – education in black history, black culture, black folklore, black literature, black liberation tactics past and present; encouraging the use of symbols of blackness: African dress, combs, figurines, art, African, West Indian and Asian manufactured produce; promoting the use of films, reports and personal contacts so as to be involved in the struggle of black peoples throughout the world; promoting better understanding and communication between parents and children and attempting to identify the factors that lead to estrangement of children from parents; seeking to improve the stability of the black family – a political programme must also include education *in the workings of the system*. This means education in the part played by colonization in British economic history; an understanding of the English local government system, the English penal system, English law and the British constitution; policies in education, housing, employment, urban renewal and immigration law. All this is a pre-requisite to assuming black representation on local government councils, boards of schools governors, management committees of youth and community centres; black representation in parliament. To the majority of blacks the Labour party is as disreputable as the Conservative party, particularly with regard to race and immigration policy. The idea of representation in parliament immediately poses the question: under which banner?

While concerning itself with political power in Britain the black movement must be as much preoccupied with Britain's foreign policy *vis-à-vis* Africa and the third world. For even after political and economic power is achieved in Britain the international injustice and inequality which keeps whole nations in economic subjugation should be the concern of black and white groups in Britain. When asked why don't they go back – as they frequently are – the black people's answer is usually 'Go back to what?' The life stories of some of the people in this book and frequent reports from those who did go back amply demonstrate that there is not much to go back to.

We attempted to answer the question 'why black power in Britain?' in terms of our own experience, understanding and analysis. The strategy presented does not in any way suggest a blue-print. We believe that the authentic brand of black power is what, from common experience as black people, the collective consciousness of black people working together makes it.

# Appendix

The Psychology of Racial Prejudice

Dr Farrukh Hashmi, M.B., B.S., D.P.M.
*Research Fellow, Department of Psychiatry,*
*University of Birmingham*

The word prejudice is derived from the Latin noun *praejudicium*, which to the ancients meant a precedent – a judgement based on previous decisions and experience. Later the term acquired in English the meaning of a judgement hastily formed, before due examination and consideration of the facts. Finally the term gained its present emotional flavour, signifying opinion (favourable or unfavourable) which accompanies unsupported judgement.

When prejudice manifests itself towards individual members of minority groups, it contains two irrational elements. Firstly, there is 'prejudgement', usually in the form of denigration. Life is short, and the demands upon us for practical adjustment are so great that we are, understandably, forced to make rough and ready judgements on people and races before we have had time to examine the evidence. But not every overblown generalization is a prejudice. Some are simply misconceptions and misunderstandings. Prejudgements may be regarded as prejudices only if they are not reversible when exposed to new knowledge. Secondly, there is 'over-categorization', a common mental mechanism. We meet one or two Japanese or Chinese and on such slight evidence form an impression of what all Oriental people are like. If, however, a person is capable of changing his opinion in the light of new information then he is not prejudiced.

Since the publication of the independent P E P[1] survey of racial discrimination in Britain, one must accept the fact that racial prejudice exists in almost all walks of British life. The survey reveals without possibility of doubt that there is substantial discrimination in Britain against coloured immigrants in employment, housing, and in the provision of certain services such as motor insurance. In summary, the survey concludes with the following observations:

In both employment and housing, many immigrants are following ways of life which do not bring them into contact with potential discrimination. There were some suggestions from people in a position to discriminate that time would reduce discrimination; familiarity would reduce hostility and make immigrants more acceptable.

Such optimism is not borne out by the findings of the research, which show the two main trends:

(1) As immigrants become more accustomed to English ways of life, as they acquire higher expectations and higher qualifications, so they experience more personal direct discrimination. This is apparent in the local differences between areas with established communities as opposed to new communities. It is reflected in the experiences of school-leavers who are the children of immigrants. Their numbers will increase.

(2) Awareness of discrimination, prejudice and hostility tends to make immigrants withdraw into their own closed communities.

Prejudice on the part of the host community, particularly those in a position of authority, is readily sensed by members of minority groups. It must be accepted, therefore, that prejudice does exist, even if it is only in the mind of the underprivileged person.

We become favourably disposed towards certain persons, objects and ideas that have become important to us during previous experience. The mildest form of emotional activity gives rise to simple 'preference', as for one colour over another. When preferences become organized and rigid they become 'attitudes'. A person may have favourable or unfavourable attitudes towards, for example, certain races, or co-education, or churchgoing. If these become fixed and not open to free discussion they acquire the force of prejudices. In some cases these may harden and become psychological complexes; in other cases deas are held with the same irrational intensity and conviction as nsane delusions. The word complex is used to refer to an attitude or prejudice that is accompanied by excessive emotion and is not open to alteration by further reasoning or logical argument.

When we speak of preferences, attitudes, prejudices and complexes we really imply that people who are of another colour, or who conform to race institutions and ideas other than those with which we are familiar, arouse in us certain favourable or unfavourable emotions based on our previous experience. In other words we are, through our upbringing, conditioned to express certain emotions. The development of prejudice is therefore a long-term process which involves many factors such as teaching by parents, and personal experience; it is a gradual process which eventually makes us dislike the people of a particular race or group. This dislike is intense, emotional, and not open to alteration through logical argument.

## THE PREJUDICED PERSONALITY

Eysenck[2] has carried out a considerable amount of work on the development of personality in relation to social attitudes. He has suggested that most people can be classified on the basis of their 'radicalism' or 'conservatism' on a scale relating to their 'tender-mindedness' or 'tough-mindedness' (the 'T' scale). He has shown that in most people prejudice is only one aspect of their more general tendency towards ethnocentrism, i.e. the belief that their own nation and social group are superior to all other nations and social groups. He has shown that people who hold anti-semitic views also tend to hold views denigrating Negroes and other nations and races, and even social classes other than those to which they themselves belong. A belief in the inferiority of women is also frequently found in anti-semites; and the same people are frequently in favour of flogging, the death penalty, the punishment of homosexuals, and against abortion law reform.

Hilgard[3] discusses a study of women college students showing prejudice and anti-semitism. The study revealed many basic personality defects among these students, including aggression induced by frustration and repressed tension. The more prejudiced girls showed a high conformity, and socially acceptable characteristics such as respect for parents, neatness, self-control and lack of sensuality. They exhibited a great deal of repressed hostility on projection tests, and an inability to express their natural impulses towards minority groups, thus justifying their own feelings of hostility.

Freud,[4] discussing the relevance of homosexuality in persecutory paranoia, advances the thesis that a homosexual impulse which has become too powerful is often dealt with by the conversion of affectionate feelings into hate, so that repressed homosexuals are likely to behave in a prejudiced manner. The development of a prejudiced personality, therefore, starts in early childhood. It is likely to develop in the kind of child who is relatively insecure in his relations with his parents who may be unduly moralistic or authoritarian. If a child is inculcated with hatred and dislike of people who are different, and if he is taught that his own values, customs, race and class are unquestionably superior to those of other people, he is likely to grow into an authoritarian personality and to have an attitude of paranoid bigotry.

Conversely, a less prejudiced and more tolerant personality is likely to have its foundations in a secure early life, and an education in which moral, religious and social values are balanced. Such a person tends to be more liberal in his outlook and to have more insight into his own weaknesses, attitudes and prejudices. Parents who forbid their children to play with the coloured children across the road or at school may be doing a great disservice to their own children and to society. It is socially important to be taught consistent values and an enlightened philosophy of life. An emotionally stable person is one who has learnt to meet and feel at ease with people of every type, colour and race. A child who has not learnt to associate with people of other races from his earliest days may not grow up into a happy and well-adjusted person in a multi-racial world.

ETHNIC OR RACIAL ?

Two points stand out above all others in the work of anthropologists. Firstly, except in remote parts of the earth, very few human beings belong to a pure stock. Most of us are mongrels (racially and genetically speaking). Secondly, most characteristics attributed to race are undoubtedly due to cultural rather than genetic differences, and should therefore be regarded as ethnic, not racial. An ethnic trait is learned, usually in childhood, and remains fixed for life, like one's regional accent. Its possessor cannot help it, and cannot help the tendency to pass it on to his children.

Freud explained ethnic group differences by the theory of basic personality structure. The theory puts emphasis on the way in which a young child learns to meet the basic requirements of life, during breast-feeding, toilet training, etc. It also stresses the importance of the mental habits and attitudes of the parents, and in particular the love and warmth found in the child's early relationship with its mother. The child's 'frustration tolerance' depends on this early training.

The innate differences in children of different races have been investigated. Pasamanick,[5] working with American Negro children, found that those living in segregated districts were more retarded in language development than white children, but Negroes and whites in mixed neighbourhoods were almost equal in linguistic ability. However, in both types of district I Q scores for Negro and white pre-school children were equal. But social factors influence verbal ability at an early age, possibly because children in segregated districts may be the offspring of less educated Negroes. There may be a parallel here with the immigrant children in Britain.

Mary Ellen Goodman[6] studied Negro and white children in a mixed nursery school. She found that

the Negro children were more race conscious than the white children. Although they were too young to understand the nature of the trouble, some of them were already in various ways defensive, over-active and tense as a consequence of their vague feelings of disadvantage ...

the young Negro children are not necessarily apathetic, slow or lazy as compared to whites. If older Negroes are sometimes comparatively slower, the reason is not to be found in their race; it is more likely to lie perhaps in their poorer health, discouragement of defensiveness against discrimination.

Chance[7] in particular amongst ethnologists has found that there is a built-in tendency in all of us (with our long evolutionary history) to withdraw from the world around us as well as from more dominant individuals (authoritarian personalities). This comes into play when an individual occupies a low social rank. Thus coloured children with the same intelligence level as their white companions may do less well academically because this inbuilt tendency disturbs their behaviour by restricting their awareness, whenever they feel they occupy a low social status in a white community.

Robert R. Sears[8] drew attention to this phenomenon a long time ago, showing how performance in a series of test situations was powerfully influenced by an individual's feelings of relative social position, rather than by his actual ability to perform the given tasks. False information given to an individual about his poor social performance in the previous test reduces his ability to explore all the information available to him in subsequent tests.

Race awareness, however, is not prejudice. A four- or five-year-old child is usually colour conscious and may therefore be aware of the difference in his race. He may well prefer those who are like himself. But it may be another three to four years (depending on his learning and parents' attitude, etc.) before this preference changes to prejudice.

When people confuse racial with ethnic characteristics, they are confusing what is given by nature with what is acquired through learning. This confusion has serious consequences because it leads to an exaggerated belief in the fixity of human characteristics. What is given by heredity can only change gradually through several generations, but what is learnt can, theoretically at least, be completely altered in one generation.

## STEREOTYPES

One must not underestimate the difficulty that a child has in constantly defending himself against being pigeon-holed into a stereotype. Most people have in their mind a picture of a typical Jew, Irishman or Indian. There are people who believe that all West Indians feed their children on cat food; that all Indians and Pakistanis are greasy and smelly; that all Jews are clever, miserly and sly. Similarly many immigrants believe that ALL English people are unfriendly, snobbish and prejudiced. These images are based on completely irrational over-generalizations. Some television programmes and children's stories contribute to this state of affairs. The golliwog in children's stories, by at least one popular author, is often depicted as an anti-social character, so it is not difficult to see how the negroid golliwog can get associated in the child reader's mind with a not-very-nice character, thereby creating a dislike of the Negro face. English children are on occasions threatened with the 'bogey-man'; this conjures up the picture of a dark-coloured stranger who takes away naughty children. Then there is the 'rag-and-bone-man' who is supposed to do the same thing, and is sometimes made to resemble a Gipsy. With stories like these, children may grow up with a fear of strangers.

Of all epithets based on visual characteristics, reference to the colour black is the most unfortunate. The word 'Negro' comes from the Latin *niger*, meaning black. Unfortunately in the English language 'black' is a word with sinister connotations: 'the outlook is black'; 'black-hearted', 'Black Death', 'blacklist', 'blackmail', etc. White signifies purity, black is for mourning. The devil and death are usually depicted in black, whereas the forces of heaven and the angels are represented in light colours. There is therefore an implied value-judgement in the very concept of 'white race' and 'black race'. Similarly the word 'yellow' has numerous unpleasant implications and this may influence our concept of oriental people.

To some extent prejudice is a function of the degree of recognizability or visibility of the group concerned, particularly in the second generation. The children of coloured immigrants in Britain are likely to face discrimination and prejudice depending on the degree of darkness of their skin. The chances are that the children and grandchildren of the West Indians and Pakistanis will still have a certain amount of prejudice against them, while the second-generation Irish children, not being visibly different, will be completely accepted because they will not fit into any of the stereotype categories.

## SCAPEGOATS

The term 'scapegoat' originated in the famous ritual of the Hebrews:

> On the Day of Atonement a live goat was chosen by common consent. The High Priest laid both his hands on the goat's head, and confessed over it the wrong-doings of the Children of Israel. The sins and guilt of the people were thus symbolically transferred to the goat, which was then taken into the wilderness and allowed to escape. The people felt better for it, and for the time being got rid of their guilt.

All people need scapegoats, and there have always been scapegoats. In Britain the Welsh in the twenties, the Irish in the thirties, the Jews and Eastern Europeans in the forties fulfilled the function. Now it is the turn of the new immigrants who incidentally happen to be of a different colour as well, and are therefore easily recognizable. Were there no one we would have to invent someone. Nowadays we are likely to label this mental process as 'projection'. We like to make someone else responsible for our own guilt, difficulties, frustrations and misfortunes. By shifting the blame on to other people we feel better. Similarly, by looking down on someone else we can restore our own shaky self-respect.

## DEGREES OF PREJUDICE

In all societies and countries of the world one can find examples of varying degrees of prejudice. In everyday life this is often expressed in the form of jokes and statements that reflect under-lying hostility and resentment against a certain group.

For example, the story is told about a Roman Catholic dig-nitary who, near Boston, offered a lift to a little Negro boy. To make conversation, he asked the boy whether he was a Catholic. Wide-eyed with alarm the lad replied: 'No sir, it's bad enough being coloured without being one of those things.'

'Thank Heavens for the coloured immigrants,' observed a Jewish friend the other day, 'people have at least left us in peace since they started coming in.'

In England during the war it was said: 'The only trouble with the Yanks is that they are over-paid, over-sexed and over here.' (Note the use of humour to allow free expression of remarks that would otherwise be hostile and offensive.)

In Hungary there is a saying: 'An anti-semite is a person who hates the Jews more than is absolutely necessary.'

In South Africa the English are against the Afrikaners; both are against the Jews; all three are against the Indians; and all four of them hate the blacks. However, in this statement we can see precisely the kind of over-generalization we warned against in the earlier part of this article. Some English people, Jews, Indians and Afrikaners do not hate the blacks, and are in fact working sincerely for equal rights for everyone.

There even exists, all over the world, what may be termed as 'generation prejudice'. Younger people treat the older generation as outsiders whom they consider to be intolerant, narrow-minded and unaware of changing trends. Whilst the older generation has tended to believe that youngsters are irresponsible, rude and often immoral.

Allport[9] has suggested five stages of prejudice, and several degrees of its actual expression:

(1) *Anti-locution* (hostile talk). People talk against a group with like-minded friends, usually in the form of jokes and 'funny' stories. Many people never go beyond this mild degree of pre-judice.

(2) *Avoidance.* If the prejudice is more intense it causes people

to avoid members of the despised group without actually inflicting harm upon them.

(3) *Discrimination*. Here the prejudiced person takes active steps to exclude people he dislikes from employment, housing, political rights, education, recreational opportunities or other social privileges such as membership of clubs, etc. Segregation is no more than an organized and institutionalized form of discrimination practised legally by common custom.

(4) *Physical attack*. Under conditions of heightened emotion prejudice may lead to acts of violence. A coloured family may be asked to leave a neighbourhood or be so severely threatened that it lives in fear. Throwing bricks through the windows of people's homes and shops, leaving burning crosses in front of their doors or beating up lone members of the disliked groups are examples.

(5) *Extermination*. When prejudice is allowed to become a sort of group hysteria, it may result in indiscriminate violence, Hitlerian genocide, massacres, lynchings. This is the extreme expression of prejudice.

Fortunately, in Britain we are still blessed with enough goodwill between people never to have gone beyond the third, or occasionally the fourth, stage. Nevertheless, there is no room for complacency because inter-racial tensions can mount with disastrous results. People who, commenting on American or other race riots, like to say that 'it cannot happen here', may well be deluding themselves. In present day society the great prevalence and intensity of hostility and conflict between social and racial groups needs no emphasis.

Harrington[10] *et al.* studied the mass hysteria and marked overexcitement of football crowds in Britain, and concluded that powerful forces of crowd psychology were implicated in threatening, provocative behaviour which led to fighting and senseless destruction. It would be easy to imagine a race riot starting from such a situation.

REACTIONS OF VICTIMS OF PREJUDICE

People who are persistently discriminated against, and are members of groups that are victimized, learn at an early stage of life to react to prejudice and hostility in particular ways. Very often living in a society that does not accept them makes people grow up with certain traits and personality scars that may be shown in a variety of manifestations.

Victims of prejudice may be constantly on the defensive, going through life with a king-sized chip on their shoulders. They are apt to look for hostile comments and behaviour that may never have been intended and which they may then attribute to prejudice. Another reaction is to develop an obsessive concern and worry about doing the right thing, always trying too hard to conform. Some, on the other hand, withdraw from the struggle of life, and the effort that is required for the process of socialization; they tiptoe, as it were, through life with the 'I-don't-want-to-be-any-trouble-to-anyone' attitude.

Some groups react to victimization by becoming sly and cunning; others take to clowning like some Negroes in America. Insults can be tolerated more easily by making a joke of them and one's self-respect can be defended by playing the clown until it becomes a habit to be a universally harmless buffoon.

Strengthening in-group ties is another method of defence against discrimination. The small Catholic and Jewish communities are usually much better organized in places where there is discrimination against them. Some people on the other hand – particularly children – may learn to defend themselves against the humiliation of being rejected by denying their membership of the minority group. They identify with the predominant group along with a kind of self-hate for having been born the underdogs, saying 'I'm not coloured and I hate all coloured people.' The next stage in this process is to join in aggression against one's own group.

One solution to such psychological conflict is to identify with the aggressor. The cruel behaviour of the Jewish guards in the concentration camps during the last world war, and the behaviour of Jewish police in the Warsaw ghetto, are interesting historical examples of this group psychopathology. It was always the policy of the Nazis to employ criminals to do their dirty work for them. They found such elements in all countries, and among the Jews. Of course the fact that a number of Jews, Frenchmen, Dutchmen, etc. were prepared to exercise brutality against their own people in order to secure favours from their Nazi masters only proves that criminals and opportunists exist among all races and in all societies.

To feel sympathy for and give precedence to one's own group is understandable and human, and yet the corollary to such a preference is to express prejudice against the out-group. Such a prejudice can change into hatred, and if that happens the out-group, either in desperation or if it feels strong enough, fights back.

· Black Muslims are a good example. The American Negroes who have suffered a great deal through slavery and discrimination find the idea of being a Muslim very appealing. Ironically, by advocating discrimination against the whites and through an inverted snobbery of asserting black supremacy, they are acting in an un-Islamic manner, for Islam advocates very strongly the equality of all human beings.

A relatively healthier method of reacting against discrimination is to make a greater effort to acquire knowledge and skills in order to reach a better position in society. Many Jews, for example, have distinguished themselves through brilliant work in science and the arts, and have thereby earned respect in certain quarters for themselves and their people. Of course, there may also be a suggestion here of survival of the fittest, the best adapted and the most intelligent Jews having been best able to survive the centuries of persecution.

Conversely, in any community increased effort and the success that may accompany it is sometimes misapplied. Successful members of the out-group often go in for symbolic status-seeking: they wear flashy clothes, buy big cars, or acquire money through devious means, by gambling, prostitution, drug-pushing, gangsterism and crime. In children and teenagers this is manifested in delinquency and vandalism, and some seek identity through group membership by joining gangs.

A person who feels rejected and incapable of making the social adjustment can deal with his humiliation either by making an extra effort (hoping to be accepted and carrying a self-fulfilling prophecy in his heart), or by becoming anxious and worried, thus reacting in a neurotic manner.

## CULTURAL ASPECTS

### (1) *Class*

Most immigrants to Britain are peasants. They are not used to living in towns. When they arrive straight from their remote villages (perhaps in the foothills of the Himalayas, or in County Clare or St Kitts), to be plunged into highly competitive and cramped life of the large industrial cities in Britain, they may feel completely lost. They inevitably and unwittingly do things that are not acceptable to their neighbours here, such as keeping chickens in their back gardens, not opening their curtains in the morning, leaving unwashed milk bottles outside their doors, and holding all-night parties. These are examples of the kinds of activity which would not be likely to endear them to their neighbours in any large city, even in their own countries. In Bradford, Birmingham or Glasgow they certainly reinforce prejudice.

The causes of social friction therefore stem partly from the mixing of peasant classes with the city-dwellers. Immigrants can find accommodation only in districts that are declining socially. The people already living in these districts are also more than likely facing a good deal of frustration and difficulty in housing, and immigrants are the obvious target against which they can direct their hatred and on whom they can lay the blame for their condition.

Many immigrants from agricultural communities and villages practise the 'extended family' system. The close family ties which result make such people prefer to live near one another, often in crowded houses or in the same street. The clannish tendency is reinforced by linguistic convenience. These 'ghettoes' cause friction, firstly because groups of coloured men and women in the street frighten some people, and secondly because the value of property goes down in such multi-racial neighbourhoods.

## (2) *Religious difficulties*

Religious belief sometimes increases misunderstanding and prejudice. This is due either to simple ignorance of other religions, or to lack of tolerance of other people's values merely on account of these being different from one's own. A proportion of the members of all religions – usually the most orthodox – is intolerant and contemptuous of all who subscribe to other beliefs. Sometimes people are unaware that certain values have a religious significance. They may, for example, find it difficult to tolerate the turbans and beards of the Sikh community. These are marks of distinction laid down by the Sikh religion, and yet some local authorities have made employment of Sikhs conditional upon their abandonment of these customs.

Certain habits of Muslims and Jews irritate some people; for instance that they eat meat only from animals killed in a ritual manner. Some people have exaggerated fantasies about the cruel and barbaric way these animals might have been slaughtered. They also speak with disapproval of the shyness and the strange dress of Muslim women, of Pakistani marriage customs[11] or the Roman Catholic attitude towards family planning and divorce.

## (3) *Inter-marriage*

Prejudice exists in most communities with regard to inter-marriage. People do not always approve of their sons and daughters marrying into other religious groups. The Asians, for instance, object partly because of religious differences and partly because of certain socio-economic attitudes. They may feel, for example, that their Western daughter-in-law or son-in-law would be disinclined to accept the responsibility of looking after them in their old age, as their Eastern children are trained to do. Similarly the host community and white parents, although not perhaps always consciously aware of the source of their objection to their children marrying a coloured person, definitely draw a line when it comes to the question 'Will you let your daughter marry a black man?' It may be because they are afraid that their neighbours will disapprove, or will not accept the children of such a marriage – the coloured races being considered inferior. Also some people like to be able to say: 'Our Johnny is the spitting image of his grandfather.' One can see how traumatic it would be if they could not say this of their children as a result of their son or daughter's having married a coloured person. This may be interpreted as a threat to one's narcissistic, yet very human, wish for immortality through one's children.

## (4) *Sex*

Sexual competition is probably one of the reasons for friction between young white and coloured males, particularly in places where there is a highly emotional atmosphere, as in dance halls. There appears to be a fantasy among white people that the coloured races are sexually more potent and therefore more aggressive. A latent fear of excessive sexual virility may also be a factor in the parents' disapproval of their daughter's wish to marry a coloured man. For example, an intelligent English mother whose daughter had decided to marry an African student came to see the author for advice and said that although she was not prejudiced, she was very concerned that her daughter's health may not stand up to it!

### SOCIAL AND POLITICAL REASONS FOR PREJUDICE

People who get left behind in life or who are afraid that they are not making the grade in an atmosphere of rapid social change are the ones who are likely to be the most prejudiced. Most members of organizations such as the Ku-Klux-Klan, for instance, are failures even in their own society. Again this process is exaggerated by factors such as ignorance, lack of education and inability to accept one's own shortcomings.

The size and density of the minority group is directly related to the amount of prejudice against it, as is the economic situation of the community. Until recently coloured people were only occasionally seen in Britain and were considered a rather quaint novelty. They became a social problem only when they began to arrive in large numbers and started competing for houses and jobs.

The upper classes can afford to be patronizing but the working classes are of necessity always on their guard against threats to their economic and social security. This threat is not always as imaginary as one might think. At times the conflict is very real. With the acute shortage of maternity beds and a large number of coloured children being born in hospitals, an English mother who has not been able to get admission can be forgiven for registering her protest. She derives little consolation from the explanation that immigrant mothers have to be admitted because of their over-crowded and unsatisfactory home conditions. Housing shortages, overcrowded schools and overworked social services can and do cause understandable annoyance to all who suffer as a result of them. These differences can be exploited by unscrupulous people who for their own ends present as racial conflicts matters which are essentially community problems (e.g. housing shortage).[12]

Immigration does perhaps exaggerate social conflicts and frustrations which already exist, but is neither the sole nor the principal cause of them. Blaming the Jews, the Negroes, etc. for all our troubles can moreover give an aspiring politician a platform and a vote-winning election issue, by providing an outlet for social aggression and by inciting cultural loyalty.

## TYPE OF CONTACT

The quality and the frequency of inter-racial contact also determines the degree of prejudice. People living in residential areas where there are very few immigrants, mostly professional and student groups, are less likely to be actively prejudiced than those living in areas with large immigrant populations.

Casual contact does not induce us to take a stand either for or against any prevalent prejudice. It is easy, emotionally speaking, to deal with one coloured family in one neighbourhood. We can either ignore them or be on nodding acquaintance. It is harder to ignore a 'residential contact' – when one is living next door to a coloured family – than if one meets them only occasionally. Many people who accept 'occupational contact' such as working with coloured men in the factory, and even having a drink with them afterwards, may be quite apprehensive about allowing a coloured family to live in their neighbourhood or allowing their children to mix with them. In terms of 'professional contact' a coloured doctor is more easily acceptable, but a coloured policeman conjures up a different image because of the different social role he plays.

The best way to reduce tension is by doing things together and by starting with a 'goodwill contact'. People usually get to know each other on a personal basis as a preliminary to allowing a change in their attitudes. But one rude neighbour can put people off others of the same race or group for a long time to come.

The extent to which a certain group gets selected as a target for prejudice and discrimination depends on its visibility, the amount of contact between contrasting groups in occupation, housing, and social life and the degree to which the economic security, self-esteem and sexuality of certain members of the host community are threatened. In short, it depends on how much fear, anxiety and guilt is generated by the presence of the alien group.

## WAYS OF DEALING WITH PREJUDICE

### (1) *Children*

All people of goodwill would like to see a world with more harmony and racial understanding. But we do not live in an ideal world, and perhaps we shall never have a world without prejudice. But those of us who would like to make it more tolerant must realize that it is sometimes too late to do very much about the attitudes of adults. It is more useful to start with children at an early age, who will then reflect the heritage that their parents and teachers have passed on to them. It is our responsibility to mould the personalities of those who are to be entrusted with the fate of coming generations. This can only be done through dedication, through hard work, and by setting an example.

## (2) *Communication*

Children, particularly immigrants who have language difficulties, are liable to misunderstand particular words which convey meanings which were never intended. The language difficulty may also cause distress because of a genuine handicap. Most intelligence tests and examinations are inevitably biased in favour of children with better verbal facility. For this reason some immigrant children are often deprived of grammar school and university education, and a great deal of frustration and unhappiness is caused. Unless intelligence tests are re-standardized to be appropriate for these children, and unless in the meantime more reliance is placed on performance tests rather than tests for linguistic ability, immigrants will continue to suffer this disadvantage. Top priority must be given to education and to helping immigrants to learn the language of their adopted country. Prejudice thrives, in the fullest sense of the word, on lack of communication. Lack of fluency in a language is the first step towards misunderstanding.

## (3) *Guard against over-compensation*

Not all well meaning people know how to go about reducing racial misunderstanding. We must analyse our own mental process if we intend to handle these difficulties realistically. We should know, for instance, whether we are subconsciously feeling ashamed of our own prejudices and, in order to conceal our guilt, trying very hard to behave as if to say 'Let us be nice to the darkies'. This is called 'over-compensation' and it leads to an attitude which is patronizing. Many do-gooders have repressed feelings of guilt regarding their own prejudices, and they do not seem able to express a critical opinion about unpleasant, anti-social or bad-mannered coloured people. They are afraid other people might think them prejudiced. If one makes a judgement on someone of a minority group, it may get interpreted as a prejudiced statement. If we are aware of this mechanism, we shall be able to give an honest opinion, as critical as necessary, of a person regardless of his colour or creed.

## (4) *Legislation*

At a legal and administrative level there should be complete equality. In a healthy society overt legal discrimination should not exist. How far should we make laws against discrimination? Does legislation make any difference in the long run anyway? One cannot force people to be nice to each other, nor can a law change people's hearts. What we can do is to legislate against open incitement by people who want to exploit the common social difficulties and frustrations for their own ends. We must ensure that we do not allow the minds of young children to be poisoned.

After intensive research, and having accepted the recommendation of the Street Report[13] that legislation should not interfere with personal and intimate relationships between people, the race relations board in Britain came out clearly in favour of legislation, in their annual report of 1966–7,[14] saying that 'voluntary effort is insufficient in itself without legislation. Nor should legislation be thought of in terms of coercion'. The stress should be on conciliation, but it is necessary to invoke the sanction of the law for the following reasons:

(a) A law is an unequivocal declaration of public policy.

(b) A law gives support to those who do not wish to discriminate, but who feel compelled to do so by social pressure.

(c) A law gives protection and redress to minority groups.

(d) A law provides for the peaceful and orderly adjustment of grievances and the release of tension.

(e) A law reduces prejudice by discouraging the behaviour in which prejudice finds expression.

It was further recommended that the Race Relations Act should not only exclude discrimination in most places of public resort, but should also be extended to cover housing, employment, financial facilities, and so on. The report pointed out that 'the effect of widespread discrimination has consequences on the whole structure and style of life of the society in which it takes place, spreading beyond the individuals who are its victims'. The belief was stated that there is no more effective way than through the law for society not only to express its disapproval of discrimination, but also to protect itself from its consequences and to mobilize opinion and voluntary action against discrimination.

## (5) *Individual treatment*

The most strongly prejudiced people who go about advocating discrimination or violence may usually be considered emotionally disturbed. They need psychiatric treatment. Many of them attach themselves to extremist organizations in order to compensate for their own inadequacies. Of course there is no treatment for those without insight into their own shortcomings and for those who do not wish to change. With more enlightenment, people can be made aware of the fact that their outlook is a pathological one and that they need help. We must try to achieve more insight into our own weaknesses and shortcomings, instead of criticizing others for their own prejudices and fallibility. Let us also accept that prejudice does exist, not only between white and coloured, but also between different coloured communities; prejudice against minority groups is a universal phenomenon.

## (6) *Moral and educational measures*

Two things stand out above all others when we are considering ways of dissolving prejudice.

Firstly there is the need for extensive public education.[16] This would involve making efforts to achieve a closer understanding of people of different cultures, mainly through getting to know them. To accomplish this we must know a great deal more about the causes of friction, and a lot more research is required into these problems.

Secondly there is a need for a better understanding of the role of aggression in human society, if only because prejudice may lead to violence, which is indiscriminately destructive of society.

On a personal level we must encourage contact and acquaintance through clubs, meetings and social activities of all kinds. There is need for more inter-cultural education and trans-cultural exchange. Mass media such as television and newspapers can help considerably. All of us should make an effort to study the cultural backgrounds of other races, the way people from other countries think and the reasons that have prompted some of them to leave their own countries and settle in Britain.

Some members of minority groups develop an interesting habit of making liberal-minded members of the dominant group feel guilty for the presence of prejudice in the community. They forget that their own people in their own communities and countries are capable of being just as prejudiced; perhaps not about colour or race, but over certain other issues such as class or religion.

In the West Indies, for example, there is prejudice against people of darker colouring. Doors are likely to open more easily to people who come from the upper classes and have a fairer complexion. In both parts of Ireland one finds considerable religious intolerance between Protestants and Roman Catholics. There is also a strong prejudice against the English, justified by arguments which are presented as though Cromwell were still alive.

Interestingly enough it would appear that hostility against the English is becoming less intense as a result of improvement in the economy of the Irish Republic. This seems to be true of many other countries previously ruled by Britain.

In India and Pakistan at the time of partition, in 1947, religious prejudice and hatred reached an all-time high. People who were normally God-fearing and quite decent either committed or passively approved of the most savage and inhuman acts of violence against innocent people of the other side. In the southern states of America, even today, people who would be very upset if an animal were cruelly treated, may at the same time wholly or partially approve of throwing bricks at a civil rights worker, or even of shooting him to kill.

## NEED TO ACCEPT INDIVIDUAL AND COLLECTIVE RESPONSIBILITY

Before we adopt a self-righteous attitude and before we start criticizing others for their prejudice, let us take a good look at our own glasshouses and – 'Let him that is without sin, cast the first stone . . .' (John, viii, 7.)

From the point of view of social consequence, much polite prejudice is harmless enough, confined to idle chatter. Human prejudice, however, can range from the mildest form of disagreement to the most cruel form of genocide. If human prejudice is let loose, one never knows how far it may go. The danger of escalation of racial intolerance is very real and there is no room for complacency particularly in times of economic depression. In our small world with better means of communication, as we become more and more interdependent, we seem to be able to tolerate the mounting friction less and less. It therefore becomes essential for every nation and for every one of us to be aware of the danger and to try to contain it at the earliest possible stages; starting with oneself, one's children and one's home.

People who say 'it cannot happen here' when discussing race riots and violence in other countries may well be deluding themselves. There is a need for each one of us to accept individual and collective responsibility for what happens in our society around us. This applies particularly to people in the academic field – the sociologists, the theologians, the psychologists, the psychiatrists, the anthropologists, and indeed, all people involved in social sciences. None of these can afford to shirk the effort required to understand and overcome the potentially destructive hatred and intolerance in the world around us.

# Bibliography

1. PEP (Political and Economic Planning), *Report on Racial Discrimination*, 1967.

2. Eysenck, H. J., *Uses and Abuses of Psychology*, Penguin, 1960.

3. Hilgard, Ernest R., *Introduction to Psychology*, 3rd edition, Methuen, 1962, pp. 169–72 and 508.

4. Freud, Sigmund, *Introductory Lectures on Psycho-Analysis*, 2nd edition, Allen and Unwin, 1929.

5. Pasamanick, B. A., 'Comparative Study of the Behavioral Development of Negro Infants', *Journal of Genetic Psychology*, 1946, no. 69, pp. 3–44.

6. Goodman, Mary Ellen, *Race Awareness in Young Children*, Addison-Wesley, Cambridge, Massachussetts, 1952.

7. Chance, M. R. A., *Conflict in Society* (Chapter: Resolution of Social Conflict in Animals and Man), a CIBA Foundation Report, J. & A. Churchill Ltd, 1966.

8. Sears, Robert R., *Success and Failure: A Study in Mobility* (Chapter: Studies in Personality), ed. Q. McNemar and Maud M. James.

9. Allport, Gordon W., *The Nature of Prejudice*, Addison-Wesley, Cambridge, Massachussetts, 1955.

10. Harrington, J., *et al.*, 'The Violent Crowd' and 'Report on Football Hooliganism', *Personal Communications* (from Uffculm Clinic, Birmingham), January 1968.

11. Hashmi, Farrukh, *Immigration, Medical and Social Aspects* (Chapter: Mores Migration and Mental Illness), a CIBA Foundation Report.

12. Burney, Elizabeth, *Housing on Trial: A Study of Immigrants and Local Government*, Oxford University Press, 1967.

13. PEP, *Anti Discrimination Legislation*, The Street Committee Report, 1967.

14. Report on the Race Relations Board for 1966–7, HMSO, 1967.

15. Hashmi, Farrukh, *Pakistani Family in Britain*, NCCI, 1967.

16. Peppard, Nadine and Deakin, Nicholas, *Immigration, Medical and Social Aspects*, a CIBA Foundation Report, J. & A. Churchill Ltd, 1966.

*(Dr. Hashmi's essay first appeared as a Community Relations Commission pamphlet.)*

# More about Penguins

*Penguinews*, which appears every month, contains details of all the new books issued by Penguins as they are published. From time to time it is supplemented by *Penguins in Print*, which is a complete list of all books published by Penguins which are in print. (There are well over three thousand of these.)

A specimen copy of *Penguinews* will be sent to you free on request, and you can become a subscriber for the price of the postage. For a year's issues (including the complete lists) please send 25p if you live in the United Kingdom, or 50p if you live elsewhere. Just write to Dept EP, Penguin Books Ltd, Harmondsworth, Middlesex, enclosing a cheque or postal order, and your name will be added to the mailing list.

Two other books published by Penguins are described on the following pages.

Note: *Penguinews* and *Penguins in Print* are not available in the U.S.A. or Canada

*a Pelican Original*

# Racial Discrimination in England

W. W. Daniel

This book is based on an authoritative report which assessed the extent of discrimination against Commonwealth immigrants in Britain and was published by P E P in 1967. The report received enormous and controversial press coverage, both because of the subject matter and because of the thoroughness and objectivity of the survey.

As written up by W. W. Daniel, the contents of the report make an important, readable, and (in the post-Powell era) timely book on a subject which is of concern to everyone.

'The report topples myth after popular myth on colour and immigration like a fast bowl hitting ten-pins ... A coloured man will need this book to use as a scourge for the white liberal conscience. And a white man will need it to immunize himself from the virus of discrimination which is now more widespread than most Britons would dare to admit publicly'
– Dilip Hiro in *The Times*

*a Penguin Special*

# The Rise of Enoch Powell

Paul Foot

Enoch Powell is the most controversial politician in Britain today. His speeches on race have had profound effects upon British politics, race relations, and the struggle for power within the Tory Party. At the time of his dismissal from the Shadow Cabinet, he had a higher rating in the public opinion polls than the man who sacked him.

Powell's views on race have shifted significantly in the past few years. In this Penguin Special Paul Foot shows how and why they have changed – and launches a devastating counter-attack.

Most of our Commonwealth immigrants entered Britain in the decade 1954–64. Yet in this period, when according to Powell's recent speeches we were building our own 'funeral pyres', there is no published record of his ever warning about the wrath to come. In fact, Paul Foot argues, his demands for immigration control and repatriation do not rise and fall with the number of immigrants – but with his own chances of political advancement.

This book critically examines Powell's whole career, and reveals some startling political conversions. Powell's opportunism on race is possibly his last and most dangerous escapade.

FEB 1 1987

DATE

DEMCO 38-297